MW01195974

Fear of Guitar

The Common Sense Approach to Playing Chords, Rhythms, Solos & LOTS OF SONGS!

Other books by Peter Mealy:
Fear of Chords
Fear of Soloing
Fear of Ukulele
Melodic Fingerstyle Guitar

© Peter Mealy, 2012

https://lrgpm8.wixsite.com/nofearbooks

Fear of Guitar

In *Fear of Guitar* you will learn chords, rhythm patterns, chord theory, lead guitar basics, melody playing, scales, fingerpicking techniques, and how to put them together to play songs in any style. You will learn how to use a capo, play songs in any key, develop your own strumming patterns, learn songs from recordings, and learn a bunch of classic tunes!

Contents

Free videos of the lessons in *Fear of Guitar* are available online at
https://lrgpm8.wixsite.com/nofearbooks

Holding the Guitar

Correct position is very important when playing the guitar. If you hold the guitar too tight, it will inhibit your mobility in changing chords positions, and if you hold the guitar too lightly, you won't get a clear, ringing tone.

Your left hand should always be curved—from your wrist to your fingers. This will make it much easier to shift to different positions on the guitar. There should be space between the neck and your palm. Every part of your hand should be curved.

The correct way to hold the guitar is to place the waist of the guitar on your right leg, and hold it in place with your chest and upper right arm. Your left arm should never support the weight of the guitar, and avoid resting your left arm on your leg. Wearing a strap is not a bad idea, even when playing seated. The strap helps the guitar hang in a natural, ergonomic position.

Tuning The Guitar, and String Names

The diagram below shows the neck of the guitar. The horizontal lines are the frets, the vertical lines are the strings, and the thick black line at the top is the nut. The nut is the slotted piece of plastic at the top of the neck that the strings go through. All of the chords and scales presented in *Fear of Guitar* will be displayed using this type of diagram. As you look at it, the thinnest string is on the right, and the thickest string is on the left.

Notice the string names and numbers. The thinnest string is the 1st string and the thickest string is the 6th string. They are named E A D G B E from 6th to 1st. You need memorize them. When you use an electronic tuner, you need to know the strings by their letter name. Knowning the string names is also fundamental to learning chords and scales up the neck. Here is a phrase that may help you to remember the letter names for each strings:
Eddie **A**te **D**ynamite **G**ood **B**ye **E**ddie.

It is important to learn how to tune your guitar with the method shown below. Tuning your guitar "manually" helps develop your ear. You should also have an electronic tuner. They are inexpensive, easy to use, and enable you to tune your guitar quickly and accurately.

Tuning Manually

Hold, and play the note at the 5th fret of the 6th string (E), and tune the 5th string (A) until the pitch matches the fretted note. Repeat for the rest of the strings as notated.

Notice that when tuning the 2nd string (B), you hold down the 4th fret of the 3rd string (G) to match the pitch.

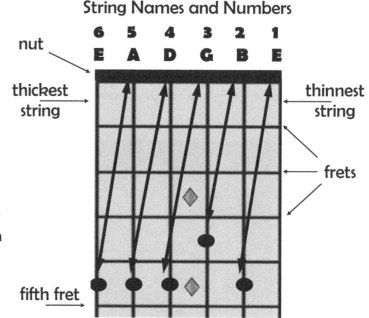

The Metronome
What, Why, and How to Use it

The metronome is an important tool in your arsenal of musical accessories that can help you maximize your practice time, and enable you to progress faster. The metronome emits a rhythmic tone, which can be set to any tempo.

When you practice a song, you need to play it slowly enough that you can play with no mistakes, and without losing the rhythm of the song. If you don't pay a song with a steady rhythm, you are not playing it musically; you're just playing randomly connected fragments.

Pick a song to practice, and find a tempo where you can play it perfectly. Slow is good. Remember – the only way to learn how to play fast is to practice slow.

Play the song with the metronome as a rhythmic guide, and when you feel completely comfortable with your chosen tempo, increase the tempo a click or two. You will find that, over time, you will be playing your tunes faster, and faster, with fewer mistakes.

Introduction to Chords
Before You Begin... *Read this!*

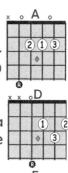

The objective of the first couple of lessons is to get you to play chords smoothly and evenly. As you move from one chord to an other, you will see that some fingers are in the same spot in successive chords. You will notice that on the A and D chord, your 1st (index) finger holds down the same note. The first finger is also on the same string for the E chord—just back a fret. So, to get through the A, D and E chord sequence, you never have to lift up your first finger. Whenever you see a note that repeats in the next chord, don't lift you finger up when you change chords. This will enable you to switch chords faster, and with less effort.

All six strings are not included in every chord. The Xs over certain strings indicate that those strings are not played in that chord. You can see that while all six strings are played in the E chord, the 6th string is not played in the A chord, and the 5th and 6th strings are not played in the D chord.

The first note that is played in most chords is called the root. The root is simply the note of the same name as the chord. The root of a D chord is a D note, the root of a G chord is a G note, and so on. When the root note of the chord is the first note that the listener hears, it sets their ear up to hear a chord that shares the tonality of the root note. Throughout this book, the root will be displayed at the bottom of each chord diagram to show on which string the root resides with this symbol: ®

Being able to identify the root of a chord will become vital as you start learning to play chords up the neck.

As you navigate through this book, you will see that each chord can come in several "colors." There are three "families" of chords: major, minor and 7th, and virtually every chord that you will encounter will fall into one of these three families. So, you may encounter a D chord (major), a Dm chord (minor), or a D7 chord (7th) in any given song. Each family provides a different "color", or mood; major chords typically sound happy, minor chords sounds sad, or melancholy, and 7th chords have a more edgy, unresolved sound.

How to Practice

Try to come up with a routine that you can follow every day. It's just like sports. You warm up, you work on technique, then you play.

When learning chords, try to keep your fingers from muting adjacent strings. Your fingers should be placed right behind the fret and press hard enough to get a nice ringing sound from each note. Use the tip of your finger, not the pad, to depress each string.

You need to develop muscle memory which will enable you to play the chord instantly. Hold down a chord, and instead of strumming it, play each note in the chord individually. If you hear a buzzing, or muted sound, adjust your finger until it rings clearly. When you are satisfied that every note is clear, let go of the chord, repeat the process. Do this ten or twenty times for each chord. This is a great way to warm up.

When you start learning songs, you will often find that certain spots are particularly difficult, and tend to derail the song. Don't practice the whole song! Isolate the trouble spots and create a repetitive exercise with them. This will be the technique portion of your practice routine. Use your metronome!

After a good warm up, and a session of dealing with trouble spots, play songs. You will find that your songs will flow a lot smoother if you warm up and work on technique before working on your songs.

Playing Chords In The Key Of A

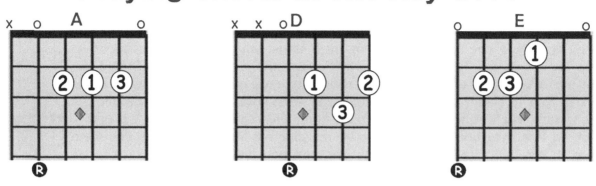

X = String is not played. O = String is played. Numbers on chord diagrams indicate left hand fingers.
1 = index finger, 2 = middle finger, 3 = ring finger, and 4 = pinky

The examples below are presented on a "staff" that is broken into units of 4 beats (or counts) called "measures." The measures are separated by vertical lines (called bar lines), and you play the chord that is notated above each measure. Start Exercise 1 by counting out loud, and strumming on the first beat of each measure. Use the second, third, and fourth beat to get your left hand positioned for the chord in the following measure. This enables you to get through the exercise without losing the rhythm of the tune. Exercises 2, 3, and 4 each add a strum on successive beats, so by the time you are playing strum 4, you will be playing a strum on every beat.

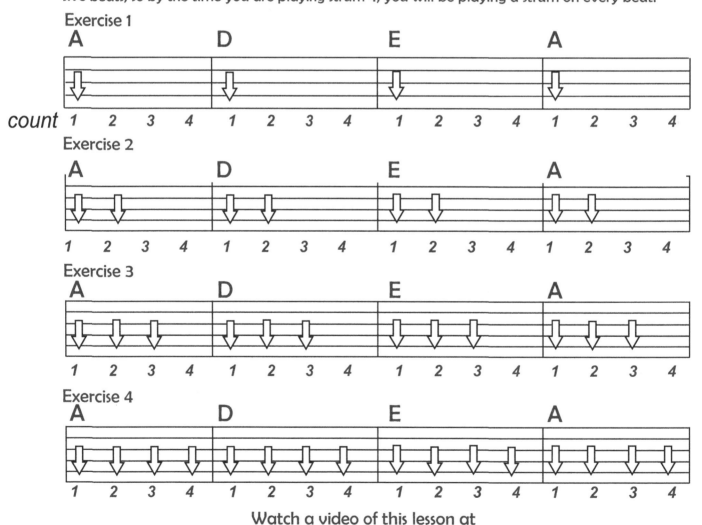

Watch a video of this lesson at
https://lrgpm8.wixsite.com/nofearbooks

Use the chords that you have learned to play these songs. Strum on the first count, and spend the rest of the measure getting your left hand positioned for the chord in the next measure. Count out loud, or in your head, and tap your foot to the beat.

Jingle Bells

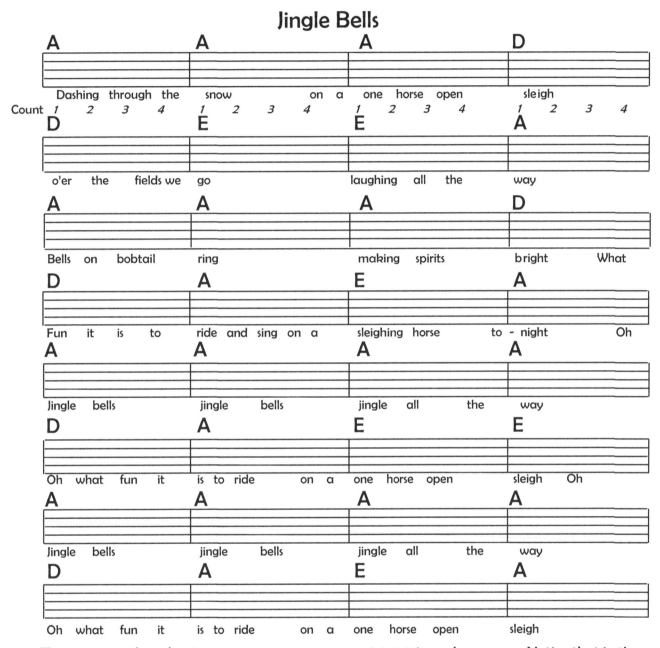

A	A	A	D

Dashing through the snow on a one horse open sleigh

Count 1 2 3 4   1 2 3 4   1 2 3 4   1 2 3 4

D	E	E	A

o'er the fields we go laughing all the way

A	A	A	D

Bells on bobtail ring making spirits bright What

D	A	E	A

Fun it is to ride and sing on a sleighing horse to - night Oh

A	A	A	A

Jingle bells jingle bells jingle all the way

D	A	E	E

Oh what fun it is to ride on a one horse open sleigh Oh

A	A	A	A

Jingle bells jingle bells jingle all the way

D	A	E	A

Oh what fun it is to ride on a one horse open sleigh

This song gets three beats per measure, so you count 1, 2 ,3 in each measure. Notice that in the 7th measure you strum the A chord on the 1st beat, and the E chord on the 3rd beat.

Happy Birthday

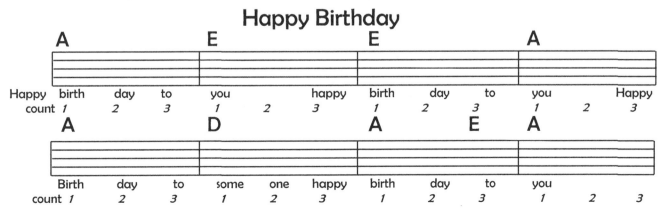

A	E	E	A

Happy birth day to you happy birth day to you Happy

count 1 2 3   1 2 3   1 2 3   1 2 3

A	D	A	E	A

Birth day to some one happy birth day to you

count 1 2 3   1 2 3   1 2 3   1 2 3

More Rhythms

Here are a few strumming patterns that will make your songs sound more interesting. For the first one, strum a downstroke on the count of 1 and the count of 3.

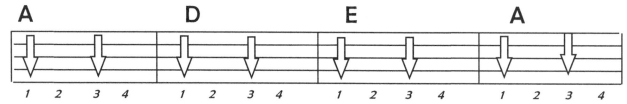

Now, add a short strum on the counts of 2 and 4. Strum all of the strings in the chord on the counts of 1 and 3. Then, hit the top strings with a very light strum on the 2nd and 4th beat. Don't strum all the way through the chord. The light strum on the 2nd and 4th beat is more of an accent than an actual strum.

You want to be able to use your strumming patterns to create dynamics in a song that mirror the emotional intensity of the vocal. You could start a tune with the strumming pattern on the 1st and 3rd beat. Then, as the song builds, you can add the light strum on 2 and 4 to add dynamics. This concept will be explored in more detail in the Embellishing Rhythms chapter.

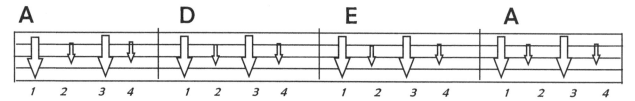

Here is a useful strum for countless pop tunes. You strum on the count of 1, then add a down-up strum on the second beat, and a down strum on the third and fourth beat.

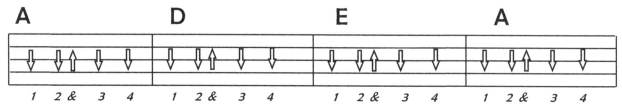

Here is a rhythm that you can use for songs that have three beats per measure. Try playing this rhythm in Happy Birthday. Use a loud strum on the 1st beat, and a softer strum on the second and third beats.

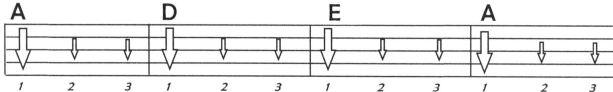

Here is the same rhythm with a down/up stroke on the 2nd beat.

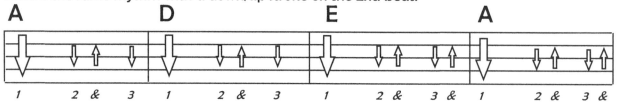

Playing Chords In The Key Of G

This lesson will introduce four chords in the key of G. There is a minor chord included in this lesson. Minor chords use the letter name of the chord followed by a small "m" while major chords are generally indicated by just the letter name of the chord. Learn these chords and practice the rhythms shown below.

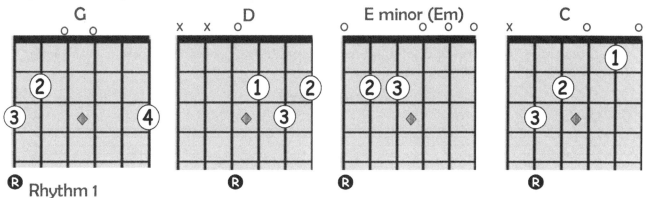

Rhythm 1

Here is a variation of one of the previous strumming patterns that has a lot of utility for pop/rock tunes. It's a little tricky with the upstroke that occurs on the & of the 3rd beat. Think down — down—up — up—down.

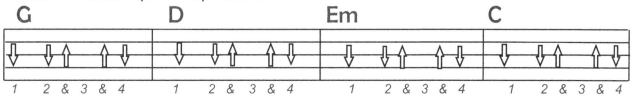

Rhythm 2

This rhythm works well on tunes with a driving rock feel. Strum two down strokes on each beat. You can change the feel of this rhythm by strumming down—up instead of all down strokes.

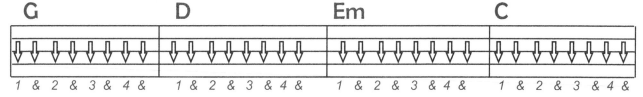

You will discover that there are a variety of ways to play most chords. Here is another way to play the G, D, Em, C chord sequence. These "voicings" are very useful in adding color to a song, and are completely interchangeable with the standard G, D, Em and C chords. Don't worry about the odd names for them. That will be explained later in the advanced chord section of this book.

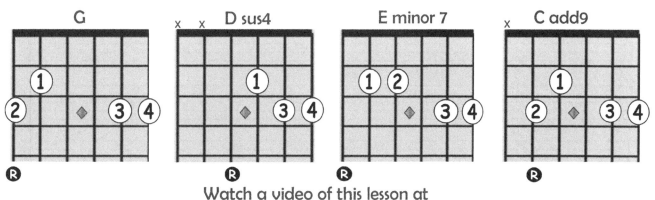

Watch a video of this lesson at
https://lrgpm8.wixsite.com/nofearbooks

Here are a couple of songs that use the chords from this lesson. Try Rhythm 1 for Wagon Wheel, and Rhythm 2 for Don't Stop Believing. Experiment with some of the other rhythms that you have learned. You can even use more than one rhythm in a song to make it sound more interesting.

Most songs are constructed with several verses and a chorus, and are arranged in verse/chorus/verse/chorus format. Sometimes a bridge is added, which typically only happens once in a song, and will use a different chord sequence that the verse and chorus.

The bracketed ‖: :‖ measures of a song indicate a repeat. You repeat that section of the song (usually a verse) before playing the next section.

Wagon Wheel

G Verse	D	Em	C

G	D	C	C

G Chorus	D	Em	C

G	D	C	C

Don't Stop Believing

G Verse	D	Em	C

G	D	C	C

G Chorus	D	Em	C

G	D	C	C

C Bridge	C	G	G

C	C	G	G

C	C	G	G

C	C	D	D

Country/Bluegrass Rhythm

This strum is great for accompanying any country or bluegrass song, or giving any song a country flavor. You will learn some variations on this strum pattern later in this book, but you can get a lot of mileage out of this basic version. It's a classic pick/strum technique that employs all four counts in a measure. On the 1st beat, pluck the 1st note in the chord (the root note). On the 2nd beat, strum the remaining notes in the chord. On the 3rd beat, pluck a bass note on a string adjacent to the first bass note. On the 4th beat, strum the remaining notes in the chord. The examples on this page show the country/bluegrass strum on the chords that you have learned thus far, but as you learn new chords, it will be pretty easy to apply this pattern to them.

To execute this strum cleanly, start by using a "rest stroke" with your pick. That is, when you strike the root of the chord on the first beat, have your pick land on the adjacent string. Don't play the string, just have your pick land on it. Then when you strum the remaining strings on the second beat, your pick will already be on the string that begins the strum. Do this on the first and third beat. It will help your accuracy.

A Chord

Play the 5th string on the first beat. Strum the remaining chords on the 2nd beat. Play the 6th string on the third beat, and strum the remaining notes in the chord on the 4th beat.

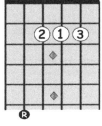 

D Chord

Play the 4th string on the first beat. Strum the remaining chords on the 2nd beat. Play the 5th string on the third beat, and strum the remaining notes in the chord on the 4th beat.

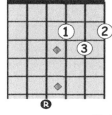 

G Chord

Play the 6th string on the first beat. Strum the remaining chords on the 2nd beat. Play the 4th string on the third beat, and strum the remaining notes in the chord on the 4th beat.

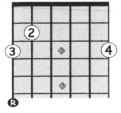 

E Chord

Play the 6th string on the first beat. Strum the remaining chords on the 2nd beat. Play the 5th string on the third beat, and strum the remaining notes in the chord on the 4th beat.

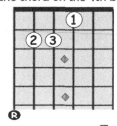 

C Chord

Play the 5th string on the first beat. Strum the remaining chords on the 2nd beat. Play the 4th string on the third beat, and strum the remaining notes in the chord on the 4th beat.

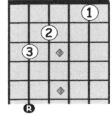 

Em Chord

Play the 6th string on the first beat. Strum the remaining chords on the 2nd beat. Play the 5th string on the third beat, and strum the remaining notes in the chord on the 4th beat.

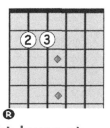 

Watch a video of this lesson at
https://lrgpm8.wixsite.com/nofearbooks

How To Play In Different Keys
The Number System

Once you have learned a few chords, you will be able to play songs in different keys. You need to be able to play in different keys so you can find the best key in which to sing a particular song. And some songs just sound better in certain keys.

The number system assigns numbers to chords in such a way that allows to you play in different keys easily, by finding corresponding chords in different keys, numerically. Here's how the number system works:

Here are the notes in the key of G: G A B C D E F#
If you give each note a number, you get:

1	2	3	4	5	6	7	1
G	A	B	C	D	E	F#	G

If you are playing a song in the key of G, using the G, C and D chords, you can refer to the chords by the numbers from that key— 1, 4 and 5.

1	2	3	4	5	6	7	1
G	A	B	**C**	**D**	E	F#	G

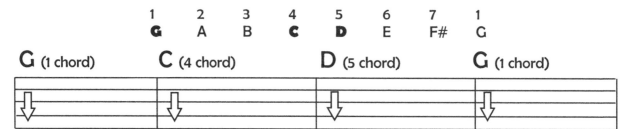

G (1 chord)   **C** (4 chord)   **D** (5 chord)   **G** (1 chord)

Now, we will apply the number system to the key of A.

Here are the notes in the key of A: A B C# D E F# G#

Just as with the key of G, you assign a number to each note in the key.

1	2	3	4	5	6	7
A	B	C#	D	E	F#	G#

So, if you want to play the original song (G, C, D) in the key of A, simply find the corresponding numbers from the original key, and substitute the chords of the same number from the new key.

	1	2	3	4	5	6	7
Key of G	G	A	B	C	D	E	F#
Key of A	A	B	C#	D	E	F#	G#

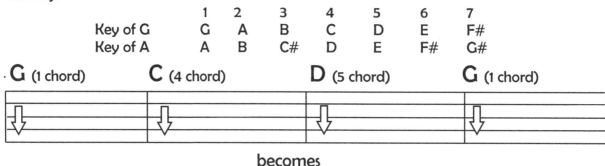

G (1 chord)   **C** (4 chord)   **D** (5 chord)   **G** (1 chord)

becomes

A (1 chord)   **D** (4 chord)   **E** (5 chord)   **A** (1 chord)

Watch a video of this lesson at
https://lrgpm8.wixsite.com/nofearbooks

The chart below shows the notes in all 12 keys. As you add chords to your vocabulary, refer to it to play songs in any key. The 12 keys are displayed in the left column, and the numbers associated with each key are notated in the rows next to each key name.

KEY NUMBERS

KEYS	1	2	3	4	5	6	7
C	C	D	E	F	G	A	B
G	G	A	B	C	D	E	F#
D	D	E	F#	G	A	B	C#
A	A	B	C#	D	E	F#	G#
E	E	F#	G#	A	B	C#	D#
B	B	C#	D#	E	F#	G#	A#
Gb	Gb	Ab	Bb	B	Db	Eb	F
Db	Db	Eb	F	Gb	Ab	Bb	C
Ab	Ab	Bb	C	Db	Eb	F	G
Eb	Eb	F	G	Ab	Bb	C	D
Bb	Bb	C	D	Eb	F	G	A
F	F	G	A	Bb	C	D	E

The 6 chord shows up in a lot of songs, and is usually a minor chord. You can use the above chart to change keys no matter how complex the chord progression.

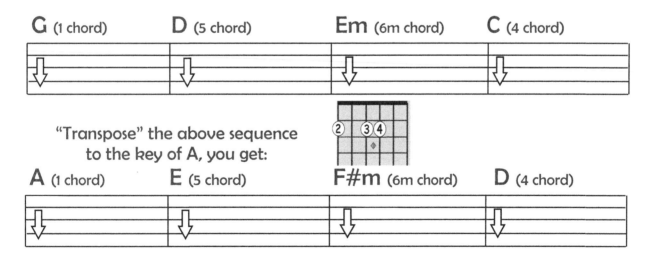

Look at the songs on pg. 103. They are all presented using the number system. As you add more chords to your vocabulary you can play them in any key that you choose.

The next two pages show the songs used earlier in this course, displayed using the number system. Practice them in different keys. The chord glossary on pg. 16 will add more chords to our vocabulary, and enable you to play in a variety of keys.

Jingle Bells

Happy Birthday

There are dozens of classic songs in the song section of this book. They are all presented using the number system, so you can choose which key to play them in. Pick a key that you are comfortable with, add some of the rhythms that you have learned, and play!

Wagon Wheel

Verse

1	5	6^m	4

1	5	4	4

Chorus

1	5	6^m	4

1	5	4	4

Don't Stop Believing

Verse

1	5	6^m	4

1	5	4	4

Chorus

1	5	6^m	4

1	5	4	4

Bridge

4	4	1	1

4	4	5	5

More Chords

You need to learn all of these chords. They are the basic chords that every guitarist needs to know, and they will enable you to play thousands of songs!

There are three types, or families of chords— Major, Minor and 7th. If a chord is just displayed by a letter (i.e. D), it is a major chord. If it is a minor chord it will be followed by a small m (D^m), and if it's a 7th chord it will be followed by the number 7 (G^7). These families will be explained in detail later.

On chords that show your first finger playing more than one string, lay your first finger across those strings. This is called barring.

An effective way to learn these chords is to identify, and play the 1, 5^7, 6^m, 4 chords in the keys of G, C, D, A, and E. These are the most widely used keys on the guitar.

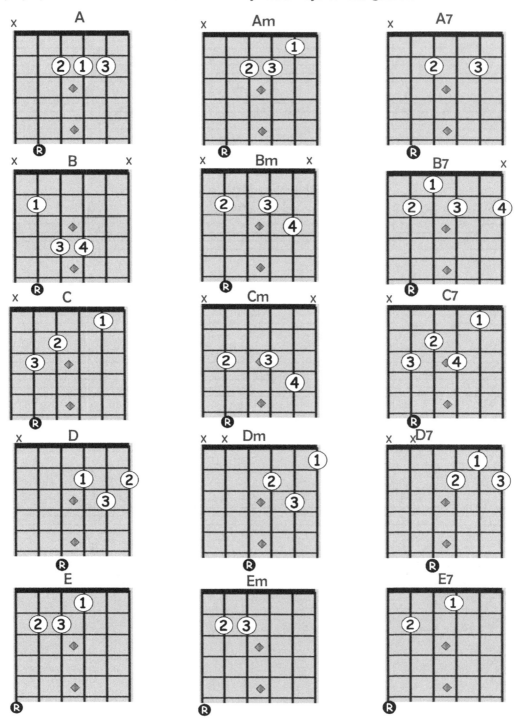

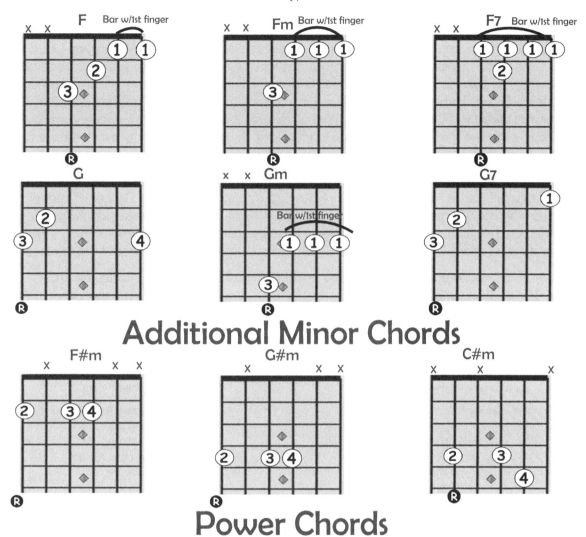

Additional Minor Chords

Power Chords

The power chord is a very useful chord that will enable you to play chords up and down the neck quickly. It is widely used in hard rock and metal tunes, but it can also be used in place of major or minor chords in any other styles. There are two power chords: one with the root on the 6th (E) string, and one with the root on the 5th (A) string. They are both moveable chords, in that, if you can identify the notes on the 5th and 6th strings, you can slide the chord shape up and down the neck, and play in any key. You can refer to the chart on page 33 to locate root notes up and down the neck.

The note on the 3rd fret of the 6th string is G so, when you play the E String Power Chord there, it is a G power chord. The note on the 3rd fret of the 5th string is a C so, when you play the A String Power Chord there, it's a C. This works anywhere on the neck. Simply identify the root note, and play the chord. The power chord is unique, in that, it is neither major nor minor, so it can be used in place of a major or minor chord, as well as a 7th.

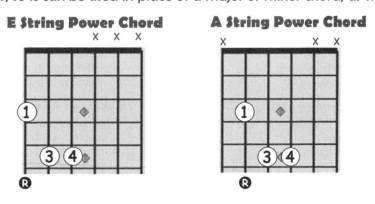

How to Use a Capo

The capo allows you to play in a variety of keys using just a few chords. When you put a capo on the guitar, you are essentially moving the nut farther up the neck, so that the neck actually ends where you put the capo. If you play a G chord with the capo on the 2nd fret, the G chord becomes an A chord, since you have moved it two frets higher than its original position. The shape of the chord is still a G, but the actual pitch puts it in A. The capo is widely used by singers who like to play the chords of a song in a particular key, but need to sing it in a different key.

The capo is also very useful when two guitarists are playing together. Rather than have both guitars pump out the same chords at the same time, one could use a capo, and play the chords on a different place on the neck. If you are playing a song in the key of G, the 2nd player could put a capo on the 5th fret and play the song in the key of D. Both guitarists would be playing in the same key, but each guitar would provide a different timbre of the same chord, making the tune sound a lot more interesting. Use the number system to find the chords in the capoed key.

The chart below shows the capo positions that you can use in various keys.

If the song is in the key of Ab,
Put the capo on the 1st fret,
and play in the key of G
Put the capo on the 4th fret,
and play in the key of E
Put the capo on the 6th fret,
and play in the key of D

If the song is in the key of A,
Put the capo on the 2nd fret,
and play in the key of G
Put the capo on the 5th fret,
and play in the key of E
Put the capo on the 7th fret,
and play in the key of D

If the song is in the key of Bb,
Put the capo on the 1st fret,
and play in the key of A
Put the capo on the 3rd fret,
and play in the key of G
Put the capo on the 6th fret,
and play in the key of E

If the song is in the key of B,
Put the capo on the 2nd fret,
and play in the key of A
Put the capo on the 4th fret,
and play in the key of G
Put the capo on the 7th fret,
and play in the key of E

If the song is in the key of C,
Put the capo on the 3rd fret,
and play in the key of A
Put the capo on the 5th fret,
and play in the key of G
Put the capo on the 8th fret,
and play in the key of E

If the song is in the key of C#,
Put the capo on the 4th fret,
and play in the key of A
Put the capo on the 6th fret,
and play in the key of G
Put the capo on the 9th fret,
and play in the key of E

If the song is in the key of D,
Put the capo on the 2nd fret,
and play in the key of C
Put the capo on the 5th fret,
and play in the key of A
Put the capo on the 7th fret,
and play in the key of G

If the song is in the key of Eb,
Put the capo on the 1st fret,
and play in the key of D
Put the capo on the 3rd fret,
and play in the key of C
Put the capo on the 6th fret,
and play in the key of A

If the song is in the key of E,
Put the capo on the 2nd fret,
and play in the key of D
Put the capo on the 4th fret,
and play in the key of C
Put the capo on the 7th fret,
and play in the key of A

If the song is in the key of F,
Put the capo on the 1st fret,
and play in the key of E
Put the capo on the 3rd fret,
and play in the key of D
Put the capo on the 5th fret,
and play in the key of C

If the song is in the key of F#,
Put the capo on the 2nd fret,
and play in the key of E
Put the capo on the 4th fret,
and play in the key of D
Put the capo on the 6th fret,
and play in the key of C

If the song is in the key of G
Put the capo on the 3rd fret,
and play in the key of E
Put the capo on the 5th fret,
and play in the key of D
Put the capo on the 7th fret,
and play in the key of C

Embellishing Rhythms

If you listen to an accomplished guitarist accompany a song, you will often hear the strum pattern change over the course of the song. Using the same strumming pattern for a whole song can prevent the song from opening up dynamically, so you should learn how embellish basic strumming patterns to help bring out the emotion of a song.

Below is a basic rhythm that was introduced earlier in this book which you play by strumming a down stroke on the counts of 1 and 3. We will use this basic pattern to add more dynamics to the rhythm.

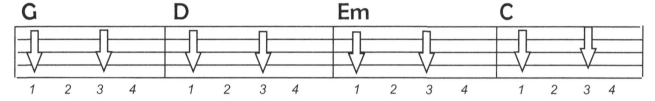

Now, add a short strum on the 2nd and 4th beat. The strum on the 1st and 3rd beat should hit all of the notes in the chord, and the strums on the 2nd and 4th beats should be much lighter, only hitting the top couple of strings. The strum on the 2nd and 4th beat provides an accent to the basic rhythm.

So, while the pulse of the rhythm is still on 1 and 3, you are adding accents on 2 and 4 to propel the rhythm. You can apply this technique to any strumming pattern

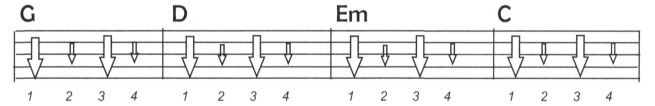

Another dynamic addition to this rhythm is to subdivide the 2nd and 4th beats to two short strums—one up, and one down.

The actual count that matches the added strums would be 1 2& 3 4&.

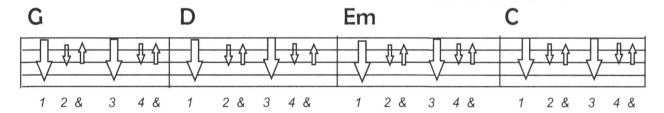

You can also use this technique in songs that have 3 beats per measure. Below you can see how the rhythm builds by using adding accents on the 2nd and 3rd beats.

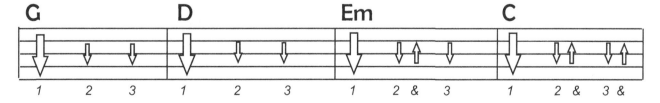

Watch a video of this lesson at
https://lrgpm8.wixsite.com/nofearbooks

Percussive Rhythm

Percussive strumming is a powerful way to strum the guitar that creates the illusion of a percussionist playing with a guitar rhythm. You can use this strum for almost any style of music.

To get the percussive "slap", let the fleshy part of your right palm drop down, and land on the strings, on the 2nd beat. This mutes the strings while your pick strikes the strings to create the percussive effect. Then, quickly follow the slap with an up-stroke of the pick on the "and" of the 2nd beat. The slap is indicated by the large S.

An alternate method for creating a percussive rhythm is to release the pressure of your left hand as you strike the strings with the pick. It's not as effective as the muted palm technique, but it's a little easier to execute.

Here is the basic pulse for percussive rhythm playing.

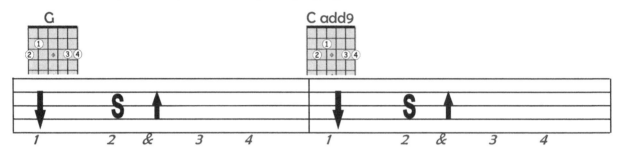

This one adds a slap on the 4th beat.

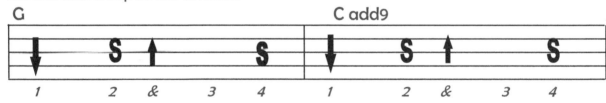

Now you can add an up stroke on the "and" of the 3rd beat to set up the slap on the 4th beat.

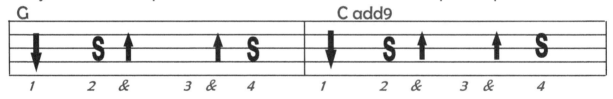

Now, add a short up stroke on the "and" of the 1st beat.

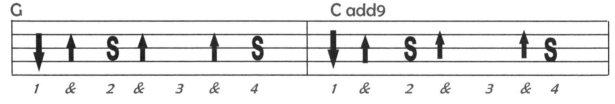

And, finally, add an up stroke on the "and" of the 4th beat, and you will have a pretty full sounding rhythm.

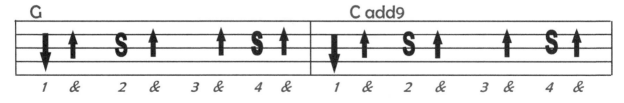

Watch a video of this lesson at
https://lrgpm8.wixsite.com/nofearbooks

Music Notation and Tablature

Reading music is a valuable skill that every guitarist should learn. This would be a good time to get a basic book on reading music and develop that skill.

Fear of Guitar will present notation using the Tablature system, as it is so widely used among guitarists. To fully grasp the tablature system, however, it will be helpful to have a basic understanding of music notation, specifically when reading rhythms.

Time Values of Notes and Rests

The symbols shown below represent notes of different time values. Different notes, and rests are allotted different time values, and the total value of the notes and rests in a given measure must equal the value of the number of beats in a measure. It's fractional. A measure of four beats can contain one whole note, or two half notes, or four quarter notes, or eight eighth notes, or any combination that totals the number of beats in the measure. All of these different time values of notes occur both in music notation and tablature.

Whole Note / Whole Rest		Eighth Note / Eighth Rest	
A whole note sustains for four beats. A whole rest is silent for four beats.		An eighth note sustains for a half beat. An eighth rest is silent for half a beat. You can play two eighth notes in the space of one beat.	

Half Note / Half Rest — A half note sustains for two beats. A half rest is silent for two beats.

Sixteenth Note / Sixteenth Rest — A sixteenth note sustains for a quarter beat. A rest is silent for a quarter beat. You can play four sixteenth notes in the space of one beat.

Quarter Note / Quarter Rest — A quarter note sustains for one beat. A quarter rest is silent for one beat.

Thirtysecond Note and Rest — A thirtysecond note sustains for an eight of a beat. A sixteenth rest is silent for an eight of a beat. You can play eight thirtysecond notes in the space of one beat.

Below you can see the fractional subdivision of note time values. The first measure contains a whole rest, meaning that there is silence for all four beats. The second measure has a whole note, meaning that the note will ring, or sustain for four beats. The thirds measure has a half note (2 beats), quarter note (1 beat), eight note half a beat, and an eight rest (half a beat). If you total their fractional value, you will get 1. The last measure, the same thing. The total value of all of the notes and rests must equal one. If you are playing a song with three beats per measure, the total value would be 3 beats.

Dotted Notes, Ties and Triplets

Here are a few other ways to express time in music notation, beyond the time value of individual notes. A dotted note extends the value of that note by one half. A ties allow you to extend the value of a note to the next note. It is represented by an arc the connects the played note to the tied, or sustained note.

The dot after the half note adds the value of a quarter note to it. You can make any note a dotted note, and extend its duration by half.

The tie allows the played note to continue sustaining for the duration of the note that it is tied to.

A quarter note can be subdivided to include 3 eighth notes. This is called a triplet, and it is sounded out as trip—el—et, or 1—e— &.

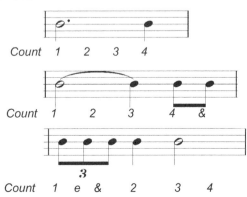

Tablature

Tablature, or TAB is a widely accepted method for notating music for fretted instruments, and is often the preferred method of notating music for fretted instrument players. It's essentially a play-by-number system that shows you which string and fret to play, numerically, without having to read traditional music notation.

The TAB staff consists of 6 lines, each one representing a string of the guitar. The top line represents the first string, and the bottom line represents the sixth string. The numbers on each line represent the frets that are to be played. Some TAB systems show only the note placement, but more sophisticated TAB systems that also show the rhythmic value of the notes, as shown below.

The sequence below shows the 3rd fret of the 5th string, and the open, 2nd, and 3rd frets on the 4th string.

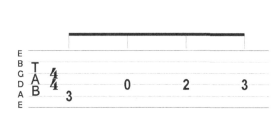

When the numbers (notes) are displayed vertically, it indicates a chord, and all notes should be played as a strum.

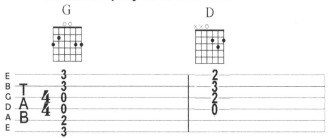

Below are the corresponding note and rest values in TAB and notation. The one idiosyncrasy of TAB is that quarter notes and half notes look alike. You have to observe where their placement is in the measure to apply the correct time value. Some TAB systems will have no rhythmic indicators.

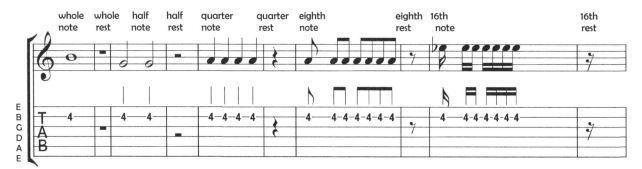

The example below shows quarter notes, triplets, eight notes, a dotted quarter note and a whole note. You can see how the rhythmic time values translate from music notation to tablature.

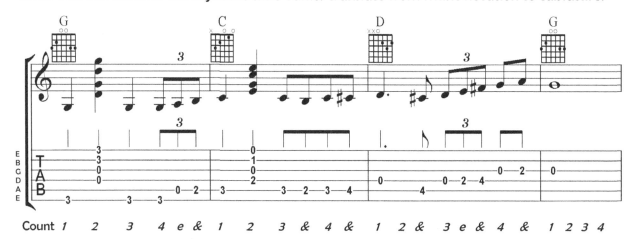

Advanced Country/Bluegrass Rhythm

The following examples show some variations on the country/bluegrass strum that was introduced earlier in this book. They use the same technique that were presented in Embellishing Rhythms.

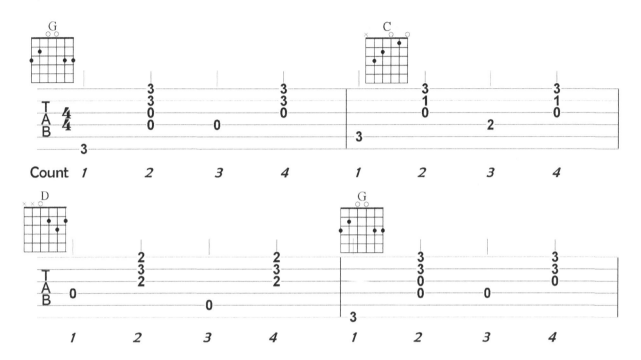

In this example, strum a down-stroke on the 2nd beat, and an up-stroke on the and of the 2nd beat, and a down-stroke on the 4th beat, and an up-stroke on the and of the 4th beat.

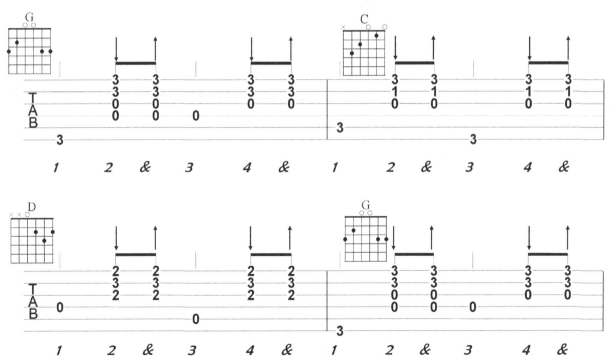

Watch a video of this lesson at
https://lrgpm8.wixsite.com/nofearbooks

The next example adds a short up-stroke on the & of the 1st beat.

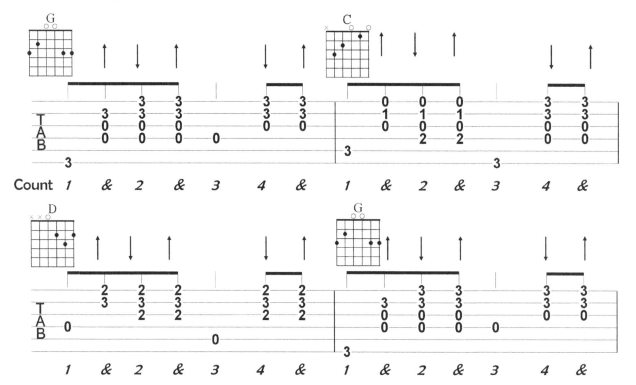

Count   1   &   2   &   3   4   &   1   &   2   &   3   4   &

You can really jazz up this rhythm by adding another short up-stroke on the "and" of the 3rd beat.

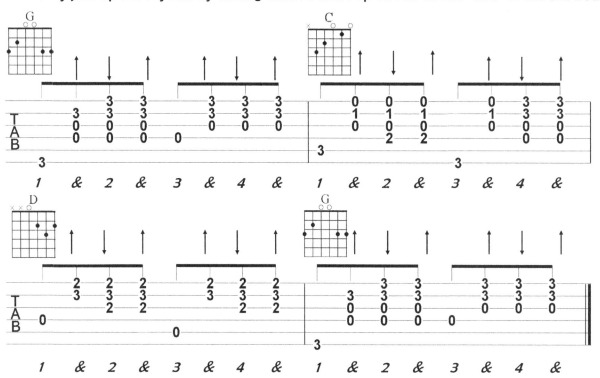

Try playing these tunes using the country/bluegrass rhythm

The Hammer-On

Hammering notes is useful technique that can add a lot of color to your rhythms. They are presented here in the context of country/bluegrass rhythm, but they are applicable in any style.

Hammer-ons allow your left hand to add some movement within the chord, while your right hand provides the rhythm. To execute a hammer-on, you play a single note, then "hammer" a finger of your left hand a fret or two above the ringing note so that a second note is heard, without picking the string again with your right hand.

In Ex. 1, pluck the open fifth string, and while it is ringing, slam your second finger onto the second fret of the fifth string. You have to "hammer" with enough velocity to make the hammered note as loud as the plucked note. You can also hammer from one fretted note to another. In Ex. 2, pluck the second fret of the sixth string with your second finger, then hammer your third finger onto the third fret.

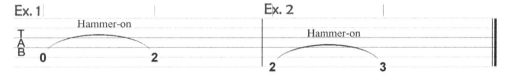

Below is an example of adding a hammered note to a standard C chord. Pick the fifth string (root) on the first beat and, strum the remaining notes of the chord on the second beat. On the third beat, lift up your second finger, and pick the open fourth string.

As soon as you play the fourth string, bring your second finger back down onto the second fret. You have to hit (hammer) it hard enough that the note on the second fret is audible. The hammered note falls on the "and" of the third beat. On the fourth beat, play the rest of the chord.

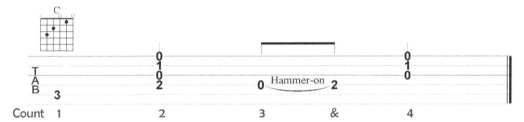

The following diagrams show where hammer-ons can be employed in standard open chords.

G Major

C Major

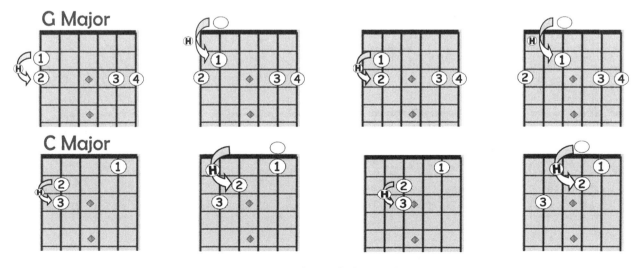

Watch a video of this lesson at
https://lrgpm8.wixsite.com/nofearbooks

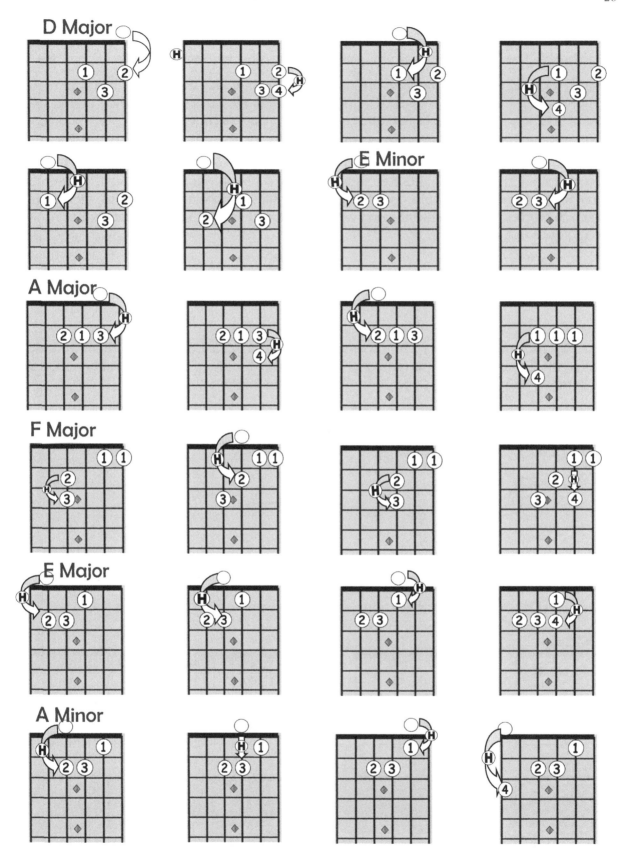

The Pull-Off

The pull-off is like the reverse of a hammer-on, in that you first pluck a note, then release it to get the sound of the note below it. You have to actually pull, or snap the string to get the sound—just lifting your finger will not produce the sound of a pulled-off note. Like the hammer-on it can be used in single note melodies, or as part of a chord.

Here is a fretted C note that is pulled off to sound an open B string, and a fretted D note pulled off to a fretted C note.

Here is a fretted G chord with a C on the second string pulled off to an open B.

Here are a few examples of pull-offs within chords.

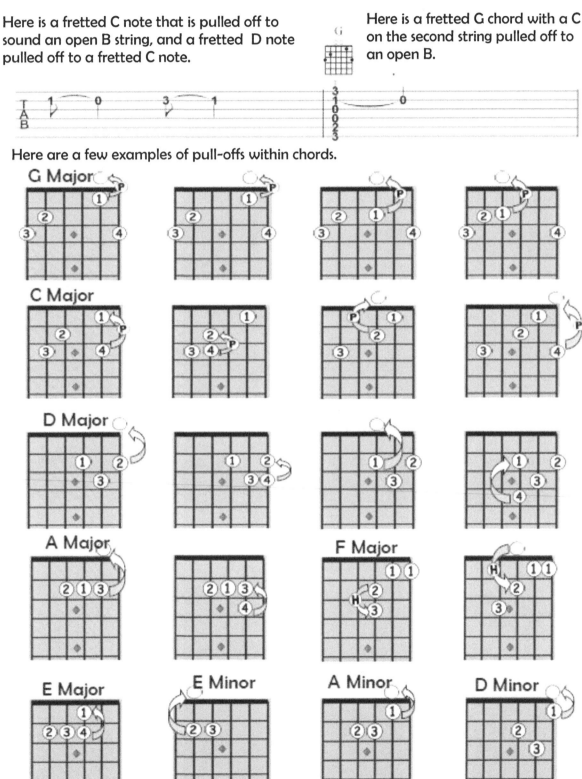

Hammer-On, Pull-Off Study

Here is a typical 1, 4, 5 bluegrass chord progression that uses hammer-ons and pull-offs to add color to the rhythm. H = hammer-on, and P = pull-off.

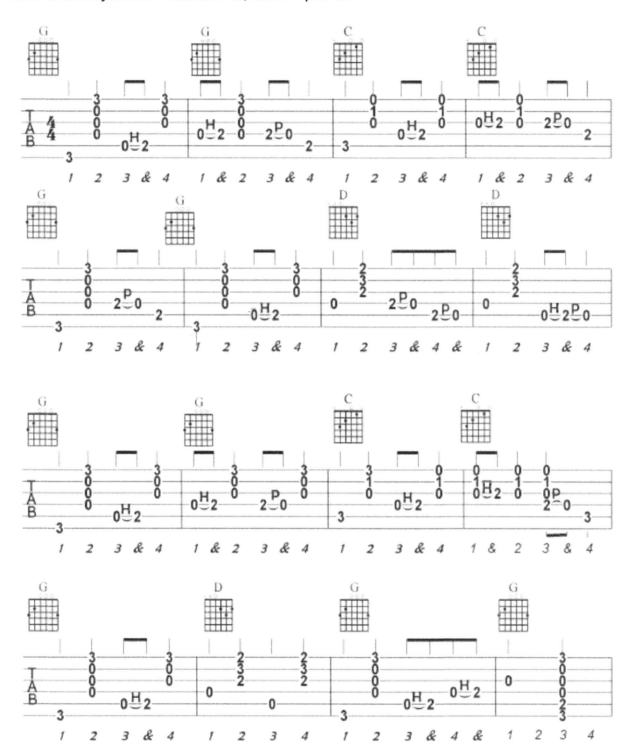

Walking Bass Lines

Walking bass is a technique where you play single bass notes to set up the next chord in a song, instead of just strumming.

In Ex. 1, play a standard bluegrass bass note/chord pattern on the first two beats, then play single bass notes on the third and fourth beats that will lead you right to the root of the C chord in the next measure.

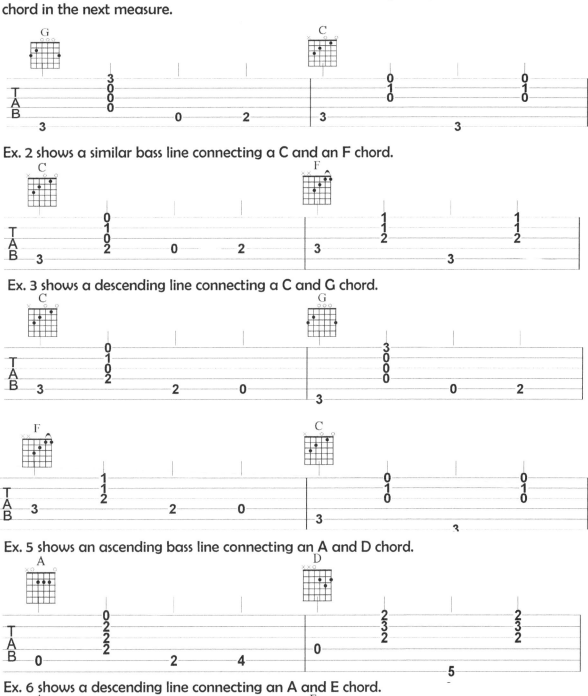

Ex. 2 shows a similar bass line connecting a C and an F chord.

Ex. 3 shows a descending line connecting a C and G chord.

Ex. 5 shows an ascending bass line connecting an A and D chord.

Ex. 6 shows a descending line connecting an A and E chord.

Walking Bass Studies

Here is a complete chord progression using walking bass lines to connect the chords.

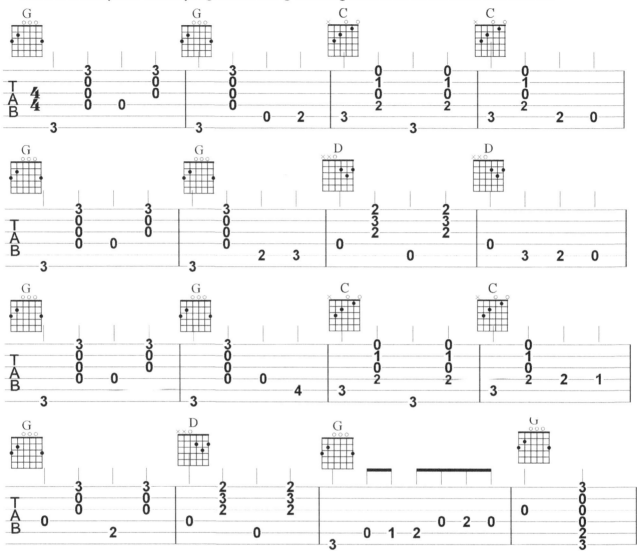

Here is a chord sequence in 3/4 time using walking bass lines to connect the chords.

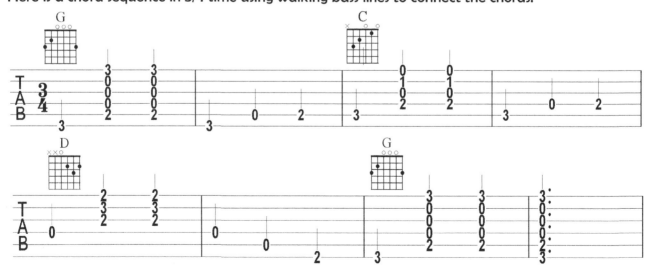

Watch a video of this lesson at
https://lrgpm8.wixsite.com/nofearbooks

Creating Rhythms

You can create countless strum patterns to accommodate different musical styles by using the concepts shown below. Try to create you own strumming patterns by expanding on these examples.

You can add upstrokes on the "and" of any beat to add rhythmic interest to your playing. Experiment by inserting an upstroke on different beats.

Example 1

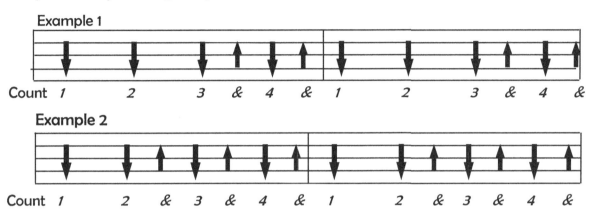

Example 2

Example 3

You can also use silences to accentuate your strums, or let a chords ring for extra beats. In the following examples there is no strum on the second beat.

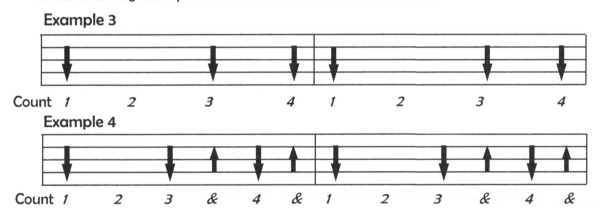

Example 4

You can also start strums on the "and" of a beat, without playing a down stroke on the preceding count. The following examples start with a down stroke on the first beat and the next strum is on the "and" of the second beat with an upstroke.

Example 5

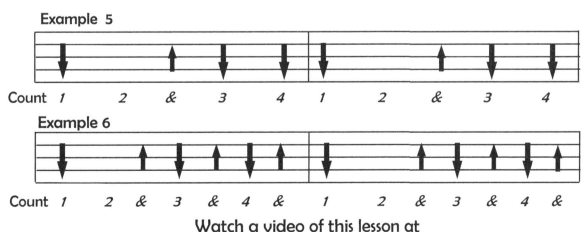

Example 6

Watch a video of this lesson at
https://lrgpm8.wixsite.com/nofearbooks

Create Your Own Rhythms

Use the blank staff paper on this page to create your own strums. Use any combination of the strumming concepts on page 30, and then see what they sound like when you play them.

Count   *1*   *&*   *2*   *&*   *3*   *&*   *4*   *&*   *1*   *&*   *2*   *&*   *3*   *&*   *4*   *&*

Count   *1*   *&*   *2*   *&*   *3*   *&*   *4*   *&*   *1*   *&*   *2*   *&*   *3*   *&*   *4*   *&*

Count   *1*   *&*   *2*   *&*   *3*   *&*   *4*   *&*   *1*   *&*   *2*   *&*   *3*   *&*   *4*   *&*

Count   *1*   *&*   *2*   *&*   *3*   *&*   *4*   *&*   *1*   *&*   *2*   *&*   *3*   *&*   *4*   *&*

Count   *1*   *&*   *2*   *&*   *3*   *&*   *4*   *&*   *1*   *&*   *2*   *&*   *3*   *&*   *4*   *&*

Count   *1*   *&*   *2*   *&*   *3*   *&*   *4*   *&*   *1*   *&*   *2*   *&*   *3*   *&*   *4*   *&*

The Notes on The Guitar

The diagram on this page shows the names of the notes on the guitar neck.

As you learn chords in different places on the neck, it will become important to learn the names of the notes to help identify those chords.

The notes on the neck fall into 2 groups: natural notes, and accidentals. The natural notes are like the white keys on a piano, and the accidentals are like the black keys. The natural notes are A B C D E F G. The accidentals are notes that occur in between the natural notes, and are referred to as sharps (#), or flats (b). There is no accidental between E and F, and B and C. So, all of the notes appear on the neck as
A A# B C C# D D# E F F# G G#.

The distance between any two adjacent frets is called a half step, and if you skip a fret, it's called a whole step.

Accidentals can be referred to as sharps or flats depending on what key you are in.

The diagram on the right shows all of the natural notes and accidentals on the guitar neck. Notice that there is a whole step (2 frets) between any two consecutive natural notes except E and F, and B and C, which only are separated by a half step (one fret).

The relationship between the natural notes, and the accidentals is the same as the relationship between the white and black keys on a piano. The keyboard shown below shows the same relationships of half and whole steps on the guitar. Sometimes seeing a keyboard can help de-mystify this arrangement of half steps and whole steps.

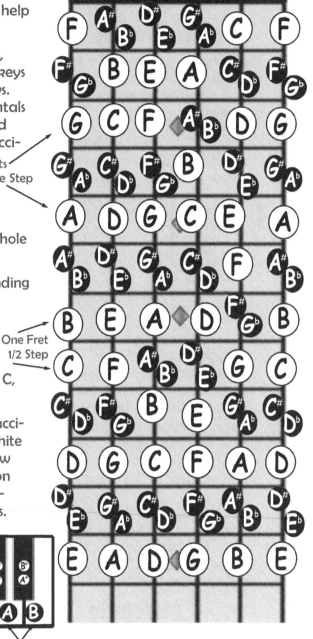

2 Frets
Whole Step

One Fret
1/2 Step

Whole Step   1/2 Step   Whole Step   1/2 Step   Whole Step

How to Memorize the Notes on the Fingerboard

- The note on the 12th fret of each string is the same as the open string.
- The notes on the 5th fret of the 6th, 5th 4th and 2nd strings are the same as the next open string, and the note on the 4th fret of the 3rd string is the same note as the open 2nd string.
- The notes on the 7th fret of the 5th, 4th, 3rd and 1st strings are the same note (an octave higher) as the previous string and the note on the 8th fret of the 2nd string is the same note as the open 3rd string.
- Pick one note and try to find it everywhere on the neck.
- Try to memorize all six notes on the 3rd fret, 5th fret and 7th fret and 9th fret. The position markers can give you a visual orientation.

Moveable Chords

Once you have a handle on all of the basic chords, they can be re-fingered, and turned into moveable chords, and played anywhere on the neck. My book *Fear of Chords* explores all of the moveable chord forms, but here we will just present the most popular moveable chords, which are based on the E and A chords.

Turning the E and A chords into moveable chords.

These chords are often referred to as bar or "barre" chords, since you "bar" your first finger across several frets to execute them. The beauty of the guitar is that once you have a chord that can be played without using open strings, you can use the same fingering to play chords in any key.

Play a standard
E major chord

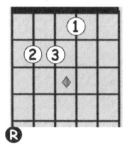

Re-finger the chord
with your 2nd, 3rd
and 4th fingers.

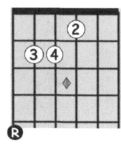

Slide the new chord up
one fret and lay your first
finger across the first fret.

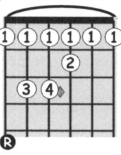

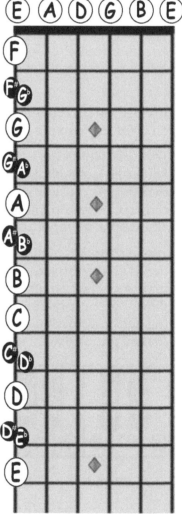

Now you have what looks like an E chord, one fret higher than the original, with your index finger functioning as the nut, or a capo. The new chord is an F chord because the root note of this form resides on the sixth string, and the note on the first fret of the sixth string is F. If you move it up so your index finger is on the third fret, you will be playing a G chord since the note on the third fret of the sixth string is a G, and so on. The fingerboard chart on the right will help you identify this chord form on any fret.

Once you can play the moveable E form, you can easily play the minor (m) and 7th chord of the E form. Once you have this chord form under control, your chord vocabulary will instantly increase by 36 chords if you factor playing a major, minor and 7th chord from the first to the twelfth fret!

7th chord using
the E Form

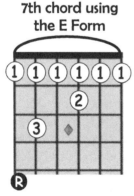

Minor chord using
the E Form

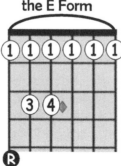

The same process of re-fingering the A form will yield another moveable chord that will enable you to find major, minor, and 7th chords anywhere on the fingerboard. Follow the same process as with the E form for turning the A form into a moveable, or bar chord.

Play a standard
A major chord.

Re-finger the
chord with your
2nd, 3rd and 4th

Slide the new chord
Up one fret, and lay
your first finger
across the first fret.

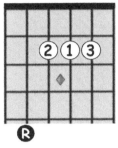 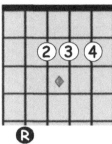 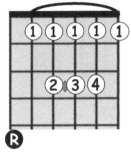 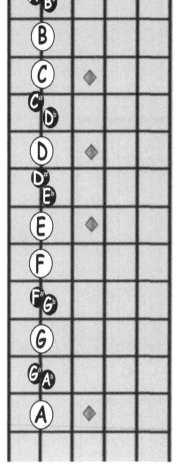

A popular alternate fingering for the A form is called a double bar. Your first finger bars across from the root and your third finger picks up all three notes, two frets higher. It's a little tricky, but it has a lot of utility.

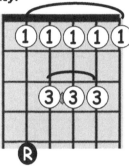

Once you can play the moveable A form, you can easily play the minor (m) and 7th chord of the A form, and your chord vocabulary will instantly increase by another 36 chords if you factor playing a major, minor, and 7th chord from the first to the twelfth fret!

7th chord using
the A Form

Minor chord using
the A Form

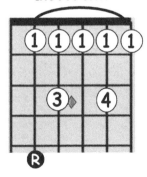 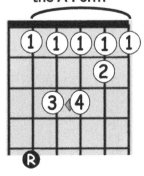

Using Moveable Chords

Using moveable chords gives you the ability to play every major, minor and 7th chord in any key, in two places on the neck.

Below is a 1 – 5^7 – 6m—4 chord sequence in the key of G. (G D7 Em C) The first example shows the basic open chords, and the next two examples show the same chords played in a couple of different positions using moveable chords.

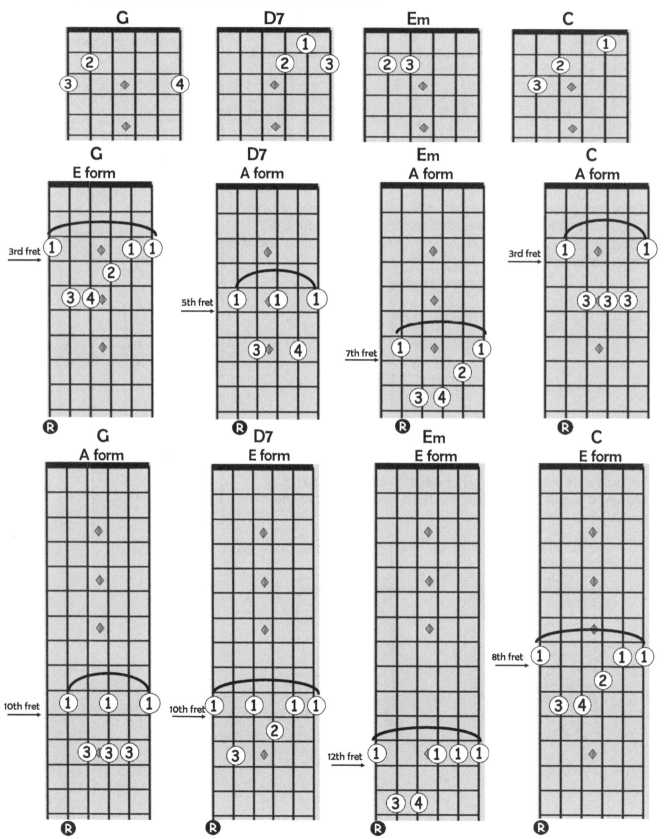

The Rest of the Moveable Chords
The CAGED System

Below you can see how the C, G, and D open chords evolve into moveable shapes. This system of chord organization is called the CAGED system, as it uses the C, A, G, E, and D chords to create chords anywhere on the fingerboard.

When you are comfortable with the five chord forms, you will be able to play any chord progression in five places on the neck. And if you consider that each of the five forms has a major, minor and 7th chord, the sum total of your chord vocabulary from the first to the twelfth fret is 180 chords!

A few of these moveable shapes don't have a great deal of utility, and they are indicated below.

In the diagram on the right you can see how the five moveable forms connect. The fingering for each form is displayed, with the root of each form highlighted in black.

The C and A forms share a root on the 5th string. The A and G forms share the chord tones on the 2nd, 3rd and 4th strings. The G and E forms share a root on the 6th string. The E and D forms share a root on the 4th string. The C and d forms share chord tones on the 1st, 2nd, and 3rd strings.

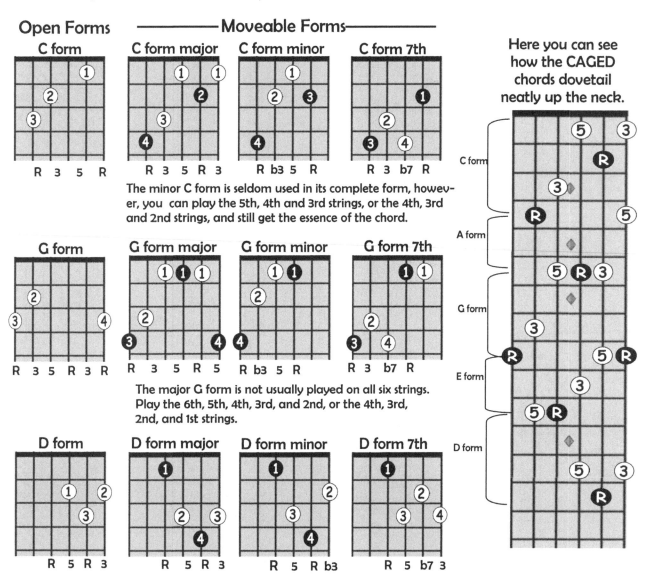

Open Forms ————— Moveable Forms—————

C form | **C form major** | **C form minor** | **C form 7th**

R 3 5 R | R 3 5 R 3 | R b3 5 R | R 3 b7 R

The minor C form is seldom used in its complete form, however, you can play the 5th, 4th and 3rd strings, or the 4th, 3rd and 2nd strings, and still get the essence of the chord.

G form | **G form major** | **G form minor** | **G form 7th**

R 3 5 R 3 R | R 3 5 R 5 | R b3 5 R | R 3 b7 R

The major G form is not usually played on all six strings. Play the 6th, 5th, 4th, 3rd, and 2nd, or the 4th, 3rd, 2nd, and 1st strings.

D form | **D form major** | **D form minor** | **D form 7th**

R 5 R 3 | R 5 R 3 | R 5 R b3 | R 5 b7 3

Here you can see how the CAGED chords dovetail neatly up the neck.

C form
A form
G form
E form
D form

Applying the CAGED System

Using moveable chords gives you the ability to play every major, minor and 7th chord in any key. Using all five forms in the CAGED system will enable you to play any M, m or 7 chord in five places on the neck, and ensure that you will never be more than a couple of frets away from the next chord, regardless of the key.

Below is a 1 - 5^7 - 6m—4 chord sequence in the key of G. (G D7 Em C) Once again, some of these chord shapes are not always useful in their complete form, but you can always play a fragment of the chord, as explained on pg. 37.

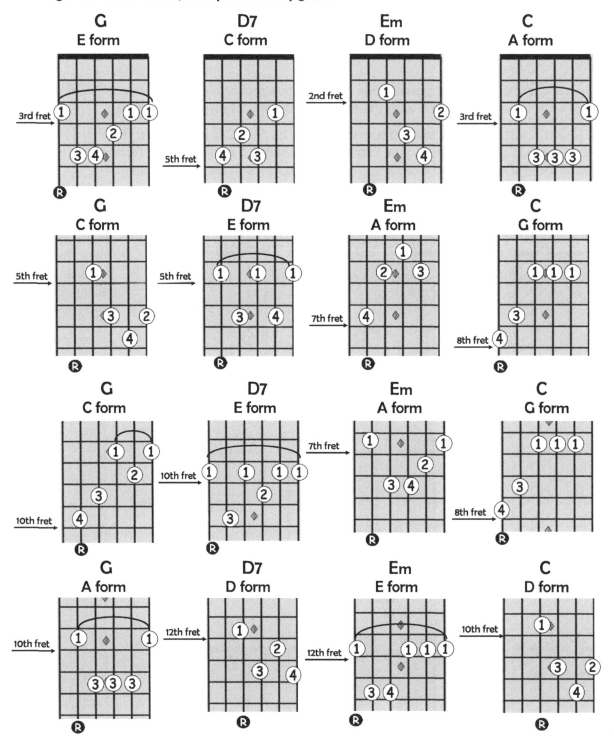

How Chords Are Made

Now that you can play chords up and down the neck, you should learn how they are created. Chords are clusters of notes extracted from a major scale. A major scale is the motor behind every key, and has that familiar *do re me fa sol la ti do* sound. Later in the book you will learn to use scales as a melodic tool, but for now you need to understand scales simply as how they relate to chords.

Here is a D major scale. The first diagram shows the letter names of the notes in the scale. The second diagram shows the same notes numerically, by scale degree, with the first note being designated as the root (R).

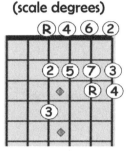

D major scale (note names)   D major scale (scale degrees)

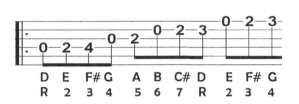

D	E	F#G	A	B	C#	D	E	F#	G
R	2	3 4	5	6	7	R	2	3	4

While there are many chords in music, they can almost all be classified by the three families that we have presented in FOG—major, minor and 7th. Each family is comprised of specific notes from its associated scale.

Major chords are created by extracting the Root, 3rd, and 5th degree from the scale. The diagrams on the right show a D major scale, with the R, 3rd and 5th highlighted in black. Once you strip away the other notes in the scale, you can see your standard D major chord.

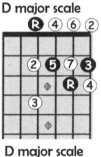

D major scale

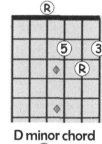

D major chord

Minor chords are created by extracting the Root, ♭3rd, and 5th degree from the scale. ♭3 means flatting, or lowering the 3rd one fret, so instead of including the 3rd degree, as in the major chord, you lower the 3rd degree by one fret. The highlighted notes show the scale degrees that are needed for the chord. You can see the ♭3 one fret behind the natural 3rd.

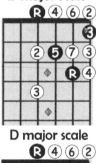

D major scale

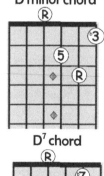

D minor chord

7th chords are created by extracting the Root, 3rd, 5th and ♭7 from the scale. Just as you flatted the 3rd degree in the minor chord, you flat, or lower the 7th degree in the scale by one fret. The highlighted ♭7 shows the note that needs to be altered to accommodate the 7th chord.

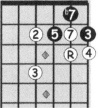

D major scale

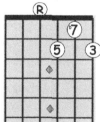

D⁷ chord

Once you understand how chords and scales are related, you can understand, and find more sophisticated chord forms, without relying on a chord book. An add9 chord, for instance, means that you play the basic major chord, count up nine notes from the root, and insert that note in the chord. A sus4 chord means that you play the basic major chord, count up four notes from the root, and insert that note.

Go back and look at the alternate G, D, Em and C chords on pg.9 and you will see how adding the 4 and the 9 makes the chord sound more vibrant. You can do this with any chord. The lesson on Extended Chords will look at these chords in more detail.

Below are the five scales for the five basic open chords. Each scale is shown with the notes by letter name, then with the major, minor and 7th chords highlighted by their numerical scale degree.

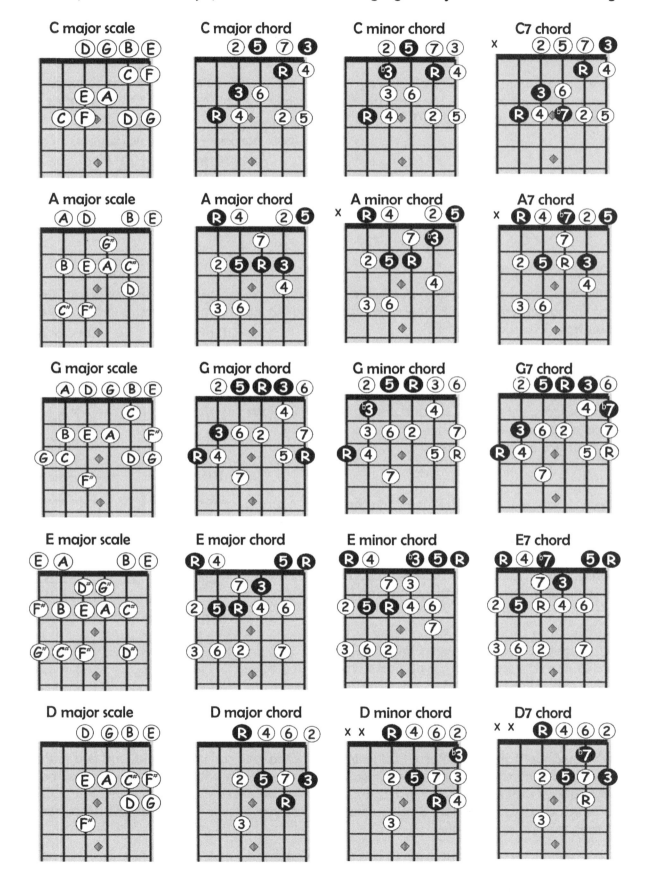

Here is the scale/chord breakdown for the moveable CAGED form chords.

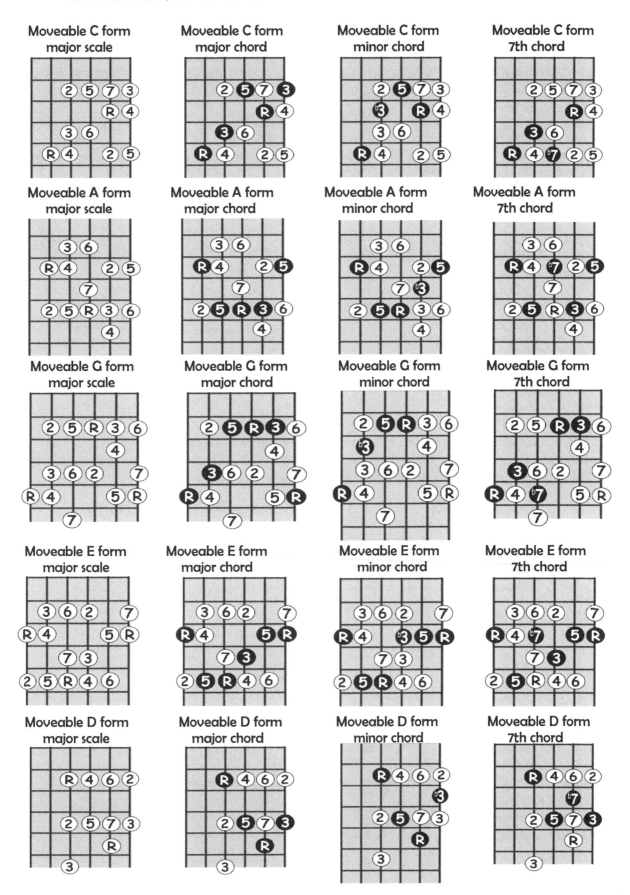

Advanced Chords

The major, minor and 7th chords are the most commonly used chords, but there are many other chords that you will encounter. Here is a look at few of these more advanced chords. The major 7 (M7) chord is a major chord with a slightly different timbre, as the m7 chord is to a standard minor chord. M7 and m7 chords are often interchangeable with standard major and minor chords. The M7 chord is created by adding the 7th degree from the associated scale, and thm7 chord is created by adding the flatted (b) 7th degree.

Major 7th Chords

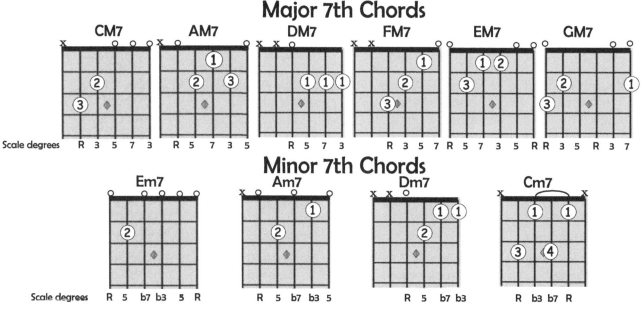

Minor 7th Chords

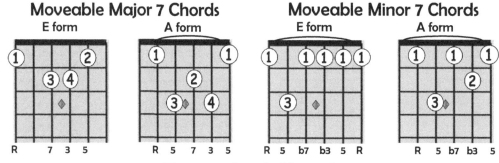

The moveable M7 and m7 chords use the same process that we used to turn the E and A chords into moveable chords. The E form moveable major and minor 7 chords have their roots on the 6th string, and the A form major and minor 7 have their roots on the 5th string, so to find a M7 or m7 anywhere on the neck, simply identify the root.

Moveable Major 7 Chords

E form   A form

Moveable Minor 7 Chords

E form   A form

Diminished Chords

The diminished (dim) chord is one of the few chords that you will encounter that does not belong to major, minor or 7th chords families. It is used as a "passing", or "connecting" chord. Every note in a diminished chord can be considered the root, so each diminished chord can be used in four different keys. The three diminished chords are : D#, A, C, F# , E, A#, C#, G and F, B, D, G#. Diminished chords repeat every three frets, so you can slide a diminished shape up three frets, and it will still be the same chord. Here are three commonly used diminished shapes.

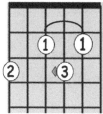
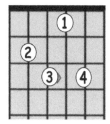

Below are two chord sequences that use some of the open and moveable major 7 and minor 7 chords, plus some of the other chords presented earlier in the book. You can use any rhythm that you are comfortable with, but a strum on the 1st and 3rd beat will work just fine.

Sample Chord Progression 1

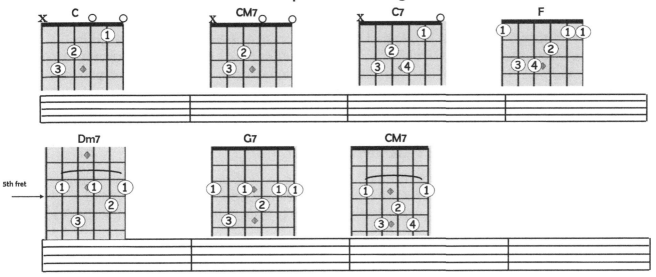

Sample Chord Progression 2

This sequence is a typical progression found in jazz tunes. There are two chords per measure, ad you should play them on the first and third beats.

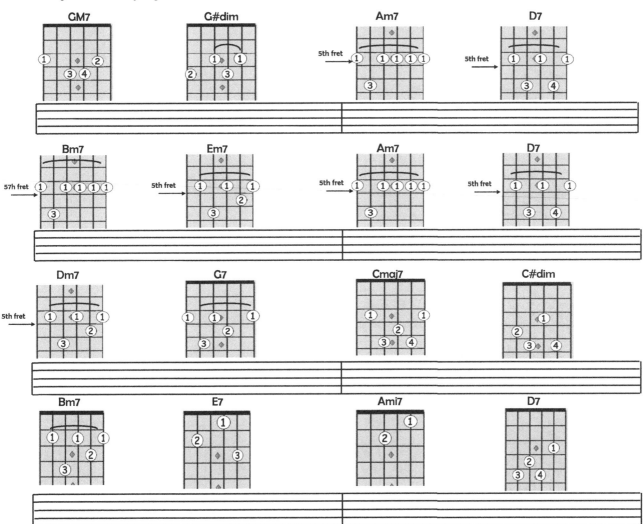

Extended Chords
sus4 and add9 chords

Earlier in *Fear of Guitar,* sus4 and add9 chords were introduced. Now that you have an understanding of scale chord relationships, the sus4 and add9 will be explained.

Anytime you have a chord that is followed by a number (6, 4, 9, 13, etc.) you simply add that degree from the associated scale. When you encounter a sus4 chord (sus is short for suspended), find the 4th degree of the associated scale, and add it to the chord. When you see an add9 chord, (sometimes called an add2) find the 9th degree (or the 2nd degree) and add it to the chord.

If you count up from the root, you will see that the 2 and 9 are the same note, just an octave apart. Sometimes one just sounds better than the other.

The beauty of the sus4 and add9 is that you don't have to wait until one appears in a song. You can substitute or add a sus4 or add9 wherever a chord appears. Their great utility is that they rarely cause any dissonance with the melody of a song; they just add some sparkle to the original chord.

Below you can see how to turn basic chords into sus4 or add9 chords by adding the 4th or 9th from the associated scale.

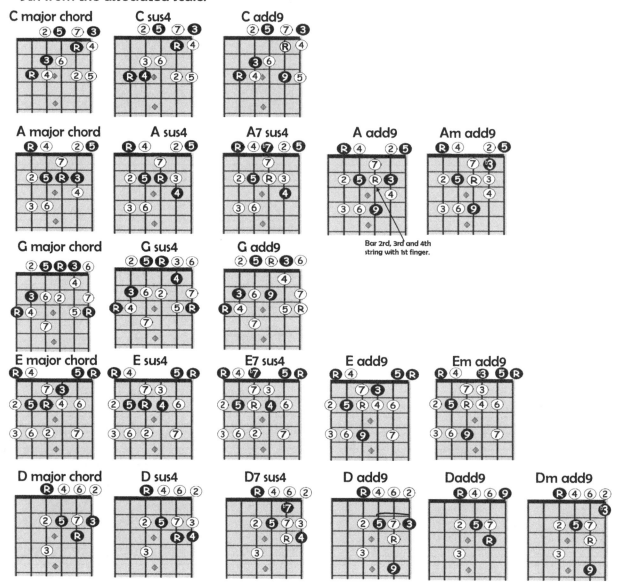

Here is how the E and A moveable forms can be turned into sus4 or add 9 chords.

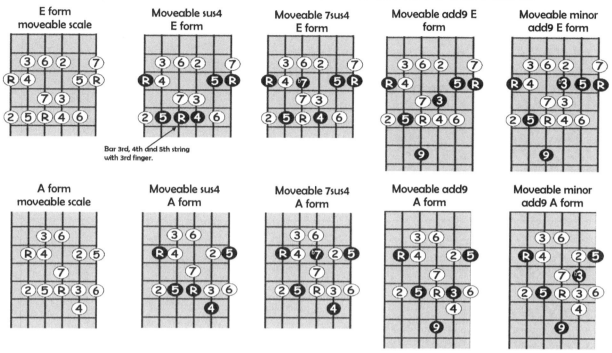

Here you can see how a basic G, D, Em, C chord sequence can come alive by turning the chords into sus4 and add9 chords. You can squeeze as many sus4 and add9 chords into a sequence as you like. The diagrams below show the left hand fingering, with the scale degrees at the bottom.

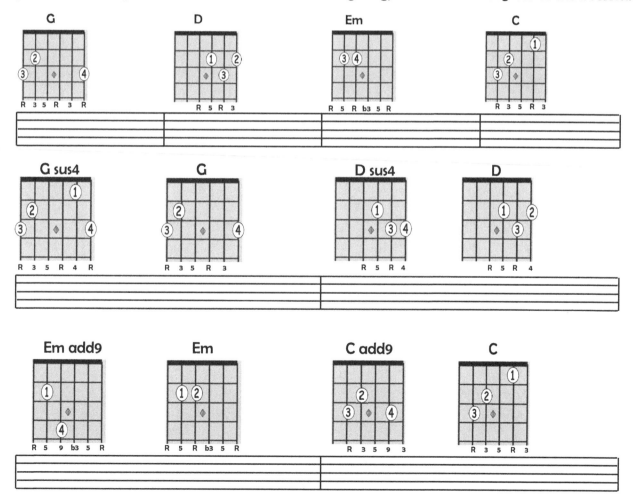

Here is the same chord sequence, but with each chord getting two measures, giving you more opportunities to insert sus4 and add9 chords.

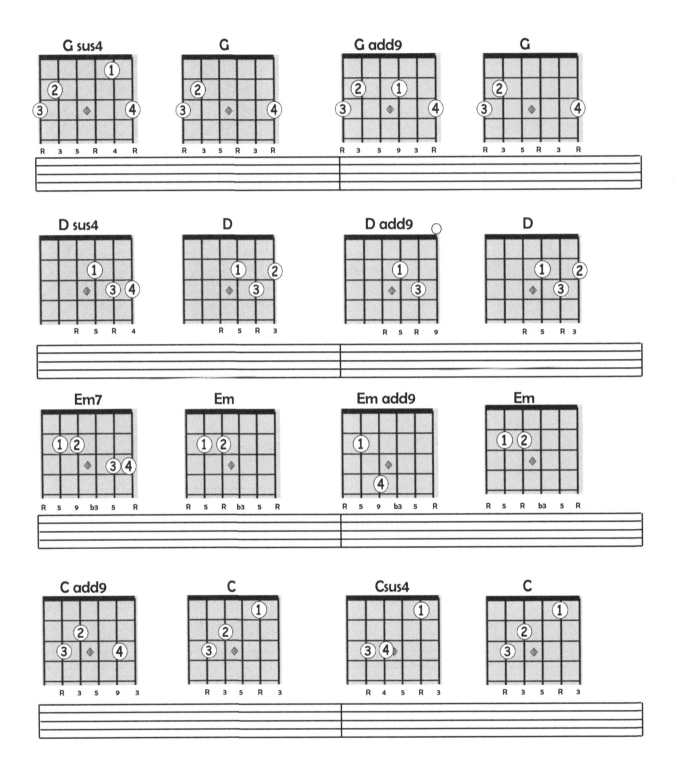

Slash Chords

Slash chords are used to create moving bass lines that connect a series of chords. A forward slash is placed after the chord's name followed by the added bass note.

For instance, C/G would tell you that you play a C chord and include a G note as the lowest note in the chord.

Just like the chords presented thus far, slash chords can be created from both open and moveable chords forms. The next few examples show some common slash chords used in familiar chord progressions, using open and moveable forms.

Here is a chord progression using slash chords in the key of C using open chords.

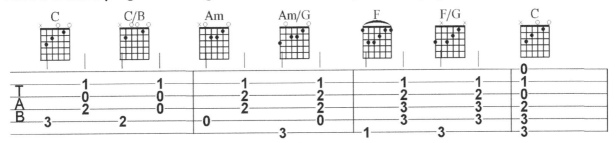

This example shows the same chord progression transformed into moveable forms in D.

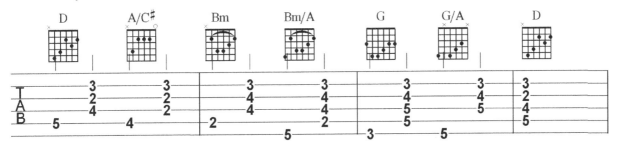

Here is a chord progression in the key of G using open slash chords.

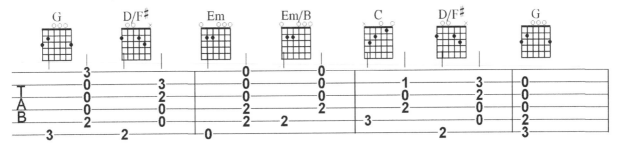

Here is the same progression using moveable chords in the key of A.

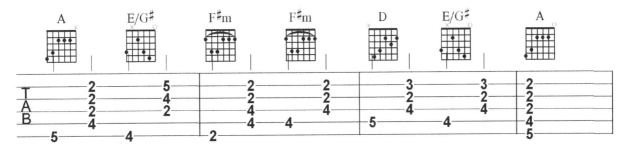

Triads and Partial Chords

Since major and minor chords are constructed of only three notes (ie. Major = R 3 5, etc.) playing a chord using all six strings means that some of the notes of the chord are doubled. If you extract the three notes necessary to create the chord, you get three note chords, called triads.

Triads can be especially useful when playing with another guitarist. The other guitarist plays the full chord, and you insert a triad. It adds a beautiful extension to the original chord without sounding cluttered. You also can use triads to add chords to a solo accompaniment. Since a triad is only three notes, a seventh chord cannot be reduced to a triad, however, you still can extract partial chords from a seventh chord that still have the character of a seventh chord, and the power of a triad.

The moveable chords introduced earlier in FOG are shown below with the triads, and partial chords extracted from them.

Major Triads

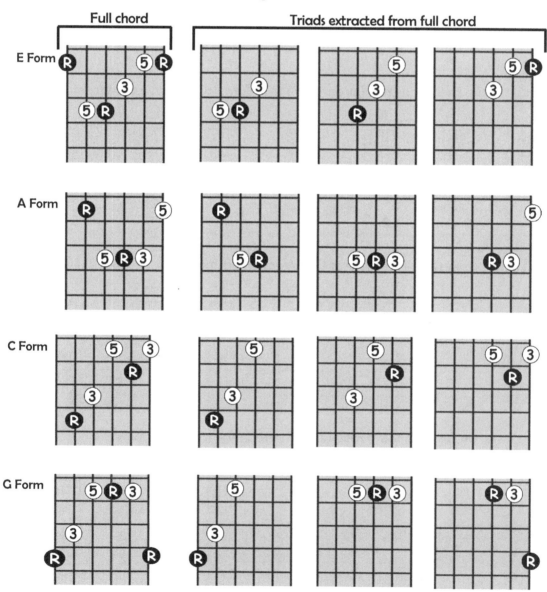

7th Partial Chords

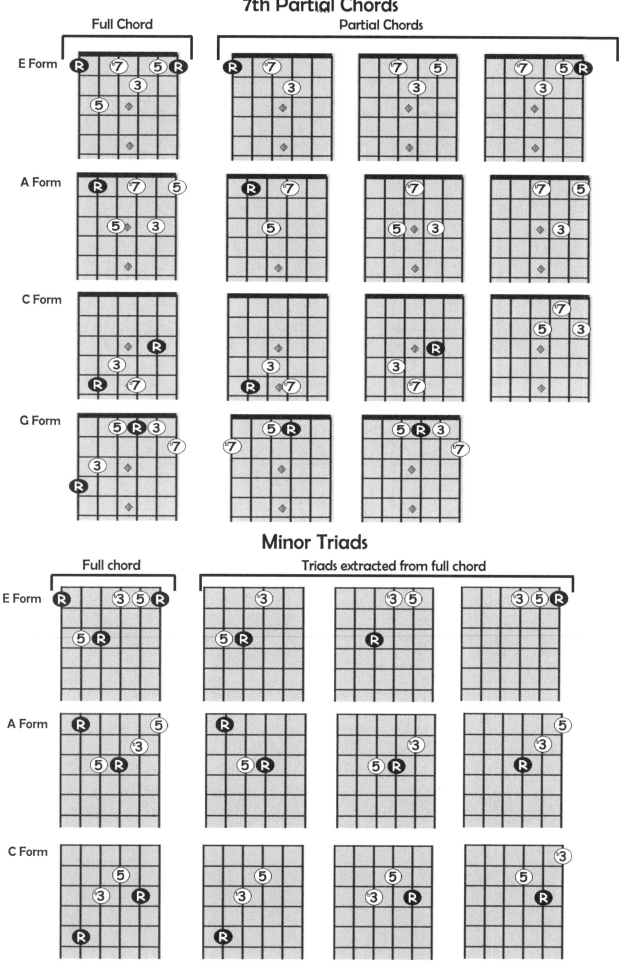

Minor Triads

You can see how the triads and partial chords dovetail up the neck via the CAGED system.

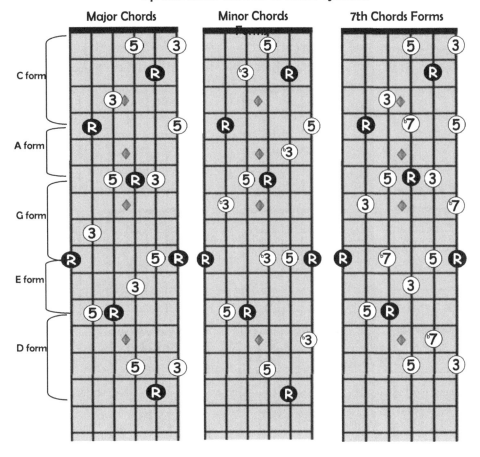

Below are a couple of examples that show how these interlocking triads can move seamlessly up the neck on different string sets (1st, 2nd, 3rd, 2nd, 3rd, 4th, etc.)

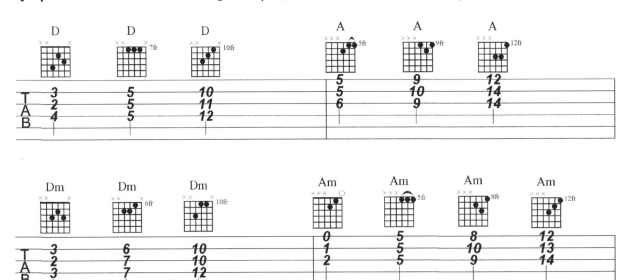

Here are two examples of adding triads to a basic chord progression.

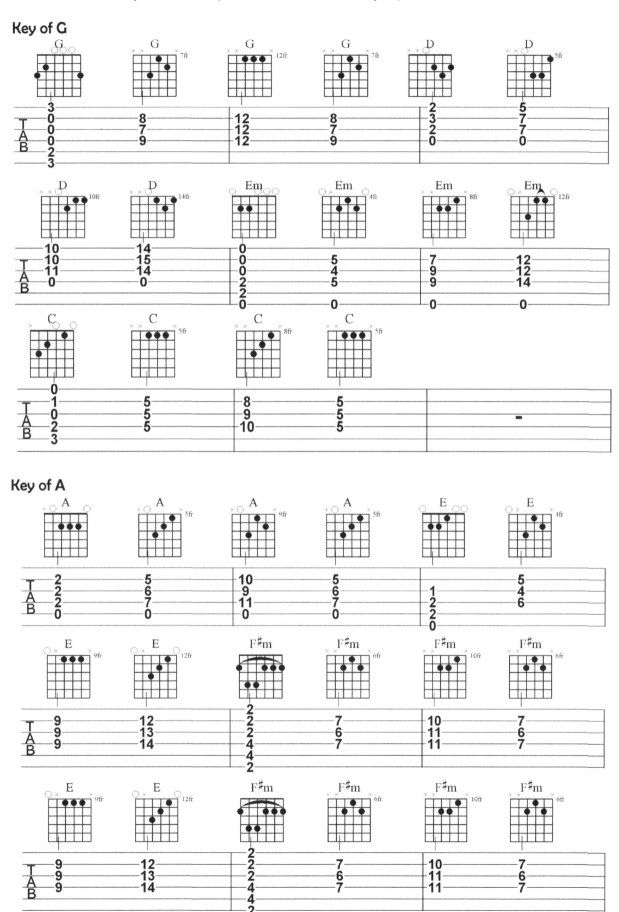

Using Intervals to Locate Chords

Understanding intervals can help you navigate through different keys, even if you are not fluent in all of the note names in a given key.

The term interval refers to the distance between any two notes. The distance between the root and the 2nd scale degree is called a second, the root and the fifth degree, a fifth, and so on. If you can identify all of the intervals in given scale, you will be able to find any chord in that key, by employing the five CAGED chord forms.

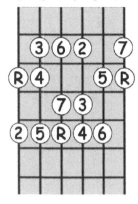

Since many songs are built around the 1, 4 and 5 chords, we'll start by showing how understanding intervals will help identify those three chords in any key.

If you look at the relationship between the root, fourth, and fifth degrees in the E form scale, you will see that the fourth is right next to the root, the fifth is over one string, and up two frets from the root, and the octave is over two strings, and up two frets. This means that the root of the 4 chord is right next to the root of the 1 chord, and the root of the 5 chord is one string over, and two frets up from the root of the one chord. If you can physically see these intervals, you can instantly find the 1, 4, and 5 chords in any key. Notice that the octave is always two strings over and up two frets if the root is on the 5th or 6th string.

The sequence below shows a 1 chord, using the E form, the 4 chord, using the A form, and the 5 chord, using the C form, or the A form.

The arrows ⤵ show the relationship of each of the chords to the 1 (root) of the scale.

The root of the 1 chord is on the 6th string, so the E form chord is the obvious choice. You could also use the G form.

The root of the 4 chord is right next to, (or a 4th above) the root of the 1 chord. The A form chord is the most logical choice.

The root of the 5 chord is one string over and two frets above (or a 5th above) the root of the 1 chord. You can use either the C form or the A form.

1 chord   **4 chord**

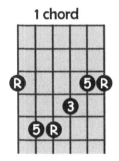
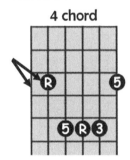

5 chord   **5 chord**

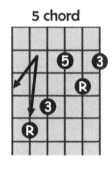
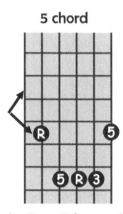

The sequence below shows a 1 chord, using the A form, the 4 chord, using the D or E form, the 5 chord, using the C or A form, and the 6 minor using the E or A form.

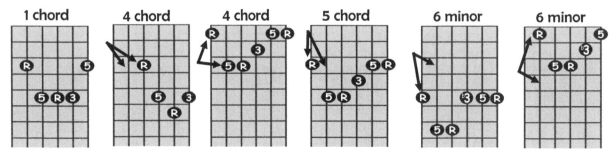

Here again is an E form major scale. The 6th degree resides on the 4th string, which would be the root of a D form chord. Notice that the 6th degree is also located three frets below the root on the 6th string, so with an E form scale, the 6th degree would be three frets lower than the root on the 6th string, and you could use an E form chord for the 6 minor chord.

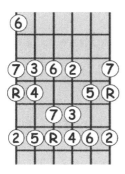

The root of the 6 minor chord is 2 strings over, and 1 fret back from the root of the E form major scale making the D form a logical choice.

3 frets back from the root of the E form major scale gives you the 6 chord—here an E form.

6 minor chord

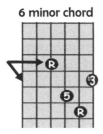

6 minor chord

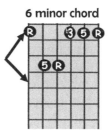

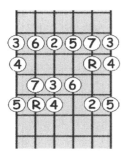

Here is a C form major scale. The same relationship exists between the root, 4th, 5th and 6th as in the previous examples. The quickest way to view the 1, 4, 5, 6 roadmap is:
The 1 (root) is on the 5th string. The 4th is on the adjacent higher string. The 5th is on the adjacent lower string. The 6th is 3 frets below the 1 on the 5th string.

The root of the 4 chord is right next to, (or a 4th above) the root of the 1 chord.

The root of the 4 chord is also back one string, and two frets below the 1.

The root of the 5 chord is back one string on the same fret.

The root of the 6 chord is 3 frets below the 1.

1 chord

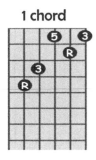

4 chord

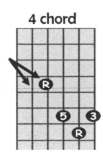

4 chord

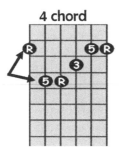

5 chord

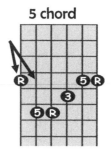

6 minor

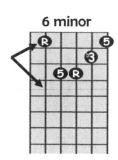

You should learn the roadmap of intervals for all five CAGED scale forms.
Once you can identify the 4th and 5th degrees of a scale, you should start memorizing the other intervals. The 6 minor chord appears in many songs, so being able to instantly identify the 6th degree will enable you to grab the 6 minor chord.

Being able to identify chord/scale degrees by intervals will also make it easy to add notes to chords. If you know where all of the scale degrees are located it will be much less daunting if you encounter an unusual chord, like a 7b9, or 13. Knowing where those degrees reside will enable you to cobble a chord together even if you have never played it before.

How to Play Melodies

Now that you have been introduced to music notation and tablature, you can start playing melodies on the guitar.

The song below is displayed in TAB, as this is such a widely used method of notating guitar music. All of the other musical examples in *Fear of Guitar* will also be presented in TAB, however, this is probably a good time to pick up a basic method on reading music on the guitar. It will benefit you greatly to develop that skill.

Once again, we'll use Jingle Bells, but you can use the technique presented here on any tune.

Notice that the chart below is in 4/4 time, meaning that there are four beats per measure. If the tune was in 3/4 time that would mean three beats per measure. Observe the note values that were presented in the last section of this book, but also use the lyrics to help you play the melody in the correct rhythm.

Playing melody on the guitar opens up a whole new dimension of guitar playing. If you have another guitarist play the chords, you can play the melody, creating a duet dynamic between the two instruments. You also may want to record yourself playing the chords, then add the melody during the playback. Apply this concept to other songs, and you will be playing the guitar!

Jingle Bells

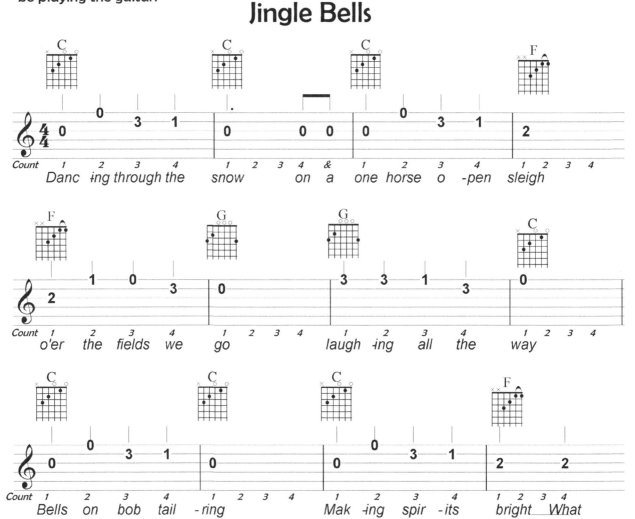

Watch a video of this lesson at
https://lrgpm8.wixsite.com/nofearbooks

How to Combine Chords and Melody

A very exciting way to play the guitar is "chord melody", which combines chords and melody to create complete arrangements, not unlike how a piano player would approach a tune.

In basic chord melody arrangements the chord is typically stated on the first beat, with the remaining melody notes in the measure played individually. You want the chord played on the first beat to sustain as long as possible, so try to leave your fingers on the chord for the whole measure. There are always a few measures that require chords played on other beats. In the following arrangement, there are a couple of measures where chords are played on the first and third beats.

The most important rule is to always keep the melody note on top. That is, as you strum a chord that contains a melody note, stop the strum when you reach the melody note.

In order to fuse the chords and melody, you have to make some small adjustments to some of the chords. The chord diagrams below will show the chords that are edited to accommodate the melody.

As you become more facile with this technique, you can start adding chords throughout the measure to support melody notes.

Jingle Bells

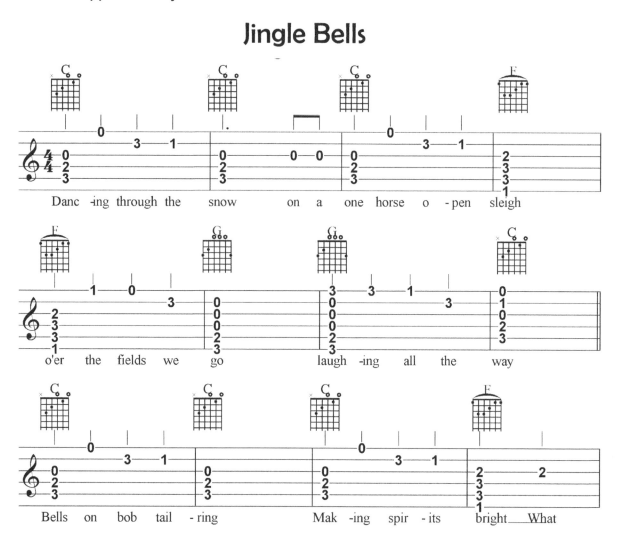

Watch a video of this lesson at
https://lrgpm8.wixsite.com/nofearbooks

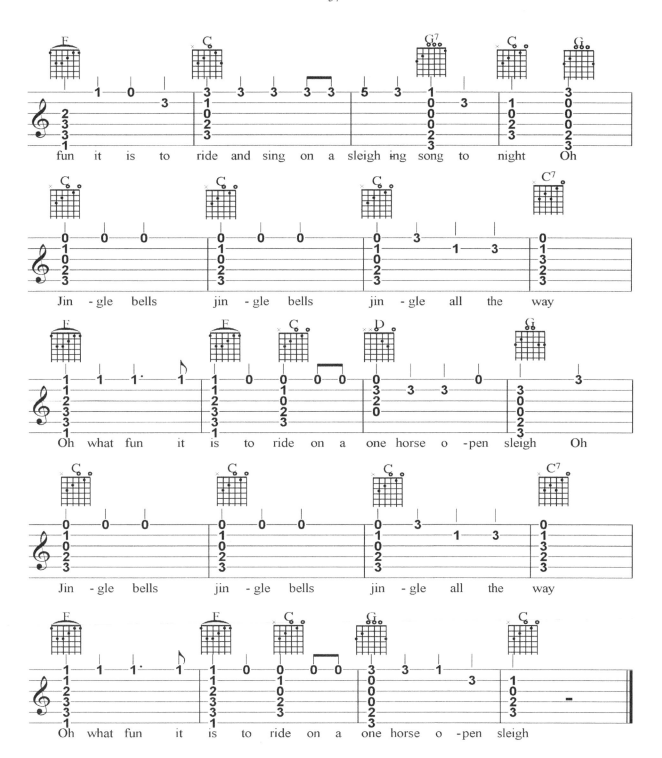

Here is *Happy Birthday*, presented as a melody, and a chord/melody arrangement. Notice that in the chord/melody arrangement, the chord diagrams have been slightly altered to accommodate the melody. Happy Birthday is in 3/4 time, so play only three beats per measure.

Happy Birthday (melody)

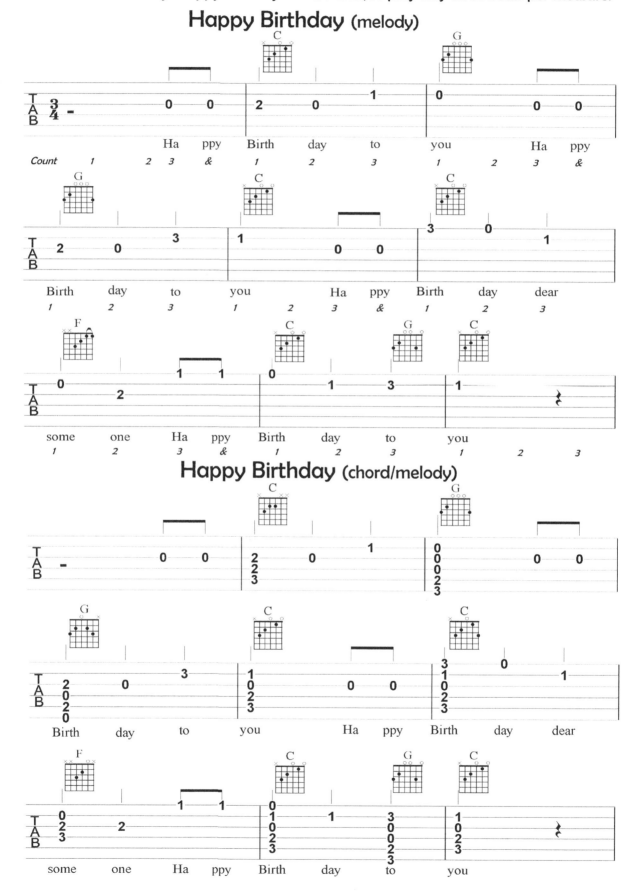

Happy Birthday (chord/melody)

Playing Chord Melody Up The Neck

You will find some melodies can't be added to chords to create chord melody arrangements because the notes are too low, and you don't have enough strings below them to insert a chord. You can sometimes put the melody in another key, or you can "transpose" the melody up an octave to allow chords to be inserted under the melody notes. Transposing an octave means to raise the notes of the melody up seven notes so that you are playing the same notes, only higher in pitch.

Let's look at a simple melody that is supported by a C and G chord. If you tried to add a chord to support the melody, you can see that you really can't insert a chord under the first four notes. There aren't enough notes.

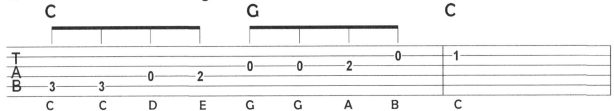

If we raise the melody up an octave, so you have the same notes, only higher in pitch, you will have plenty of room to insert a chord to support the melody. The only problem is that the melody now moves up the neck in way that it would be difficult to hold a chord down while you played the melody notes.

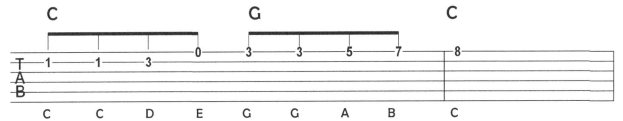

The beauty of the guitar is that you can find the same note in several places on the neck. So, we'll try to find the same notes in a more manageable array.

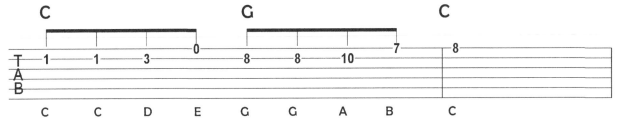

Now the notes sit in places where we can insert standard chords to support them. The first four notes sit right on top of a basic C chord, the next four sit on top of a G chord using the C form, and the last note is the top note of a C chord using the E form.

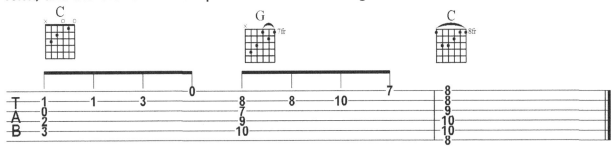

12 Bar Blues, Rock & Roll, and Jamming

This chord progression below is called a 12 Bar Blues, and it is a very important chord sequence to learn. It's called a 12 Bar Blues because unlike most other song forms, it is 12 measures (bars) long. It is a fundamental chord progression in rock and roll. The blues chord progression uses the 1, 4 and 5 chords with all of the chords treated as 7th chords.

Hundreds of blues and blues/rock songs use this progression, and once you learn it you can play them all! Try using the Percussive Rhythm for this progression.

This section will also give you an introduction to jamming. Playing music with other people is one of the joys of playing music, and this section will present some tools that will enable you to jam with other guitarists, where each player performs a different function to create an ensemble. One player can play the basic chords, one player can add some funky rhythms, and one player can play lead solos over the rhythm.

The basis for this exercise is the 12 bar blues progression displayed below. You can use any rhythm you like, but a percussive rhythm, or driving down stroke rhythm works well.

12 Bar Blues Progression

A7	D7	A7	A7

D7	D7	A7	A7

E7	D7	A7	E7 (A7)

Last time through the form, end on an A7 (1) chord.

All of these songs use the 12 bar blues progression.

Pride and Joy	Stormy Monday	Rt. 66
Cross Road Blues	Sweet Home Chicago	Red House
Love Struck Baby	Steamroller Blues	Johnny B. Goode

Sometimes 12 bar blues songs don't use the 4 chord in the second measure, and just continue pumping the 1 chord for the first 4 measures. Love Struck Baby, Pride and Joy, and Johnny B. Goode are examples of this slight variation.

Here are the 12 bar blues chords in several other keys.

	KEY	1^7	4^7	5^7
Original Key:	A	A7	D7	E7
Transposed Keys:	E	E7	A7	B7
	D	D7	G7	A7
	G	G7	C7	D7
	C	C7	F7	G7

Watch a video of this lesson at
https://lrgpm8.wixsite.com/nofearbooks

Rock and Roll Rhythm Vamp

Once you are comfortable with the 12 bar blues chord sequence, you should learn the pattern that is shown in the TAB below. It is called a vamp, and it is a moving pattern that departs from the full chord, using only two strings, and two fingers. This pattern can be played in lieu of the full chords, or played along with a second guitarist who is playing the standard chords.

Place your 1st finger on the 2nd fret of the fourth string. Then play the open 5th and 4th strings simultaneously, two times. Then, put your 3rd finger on the 4th fret of the 4th string, and play the open 5th string, and the 4th string two times. This is the vamp for the A chord. Move the pattern to the 3rd and fourth strings for D, and the 5th and 6th strings for E.

You can use down and up strokes or all down strokes to play this pattern.

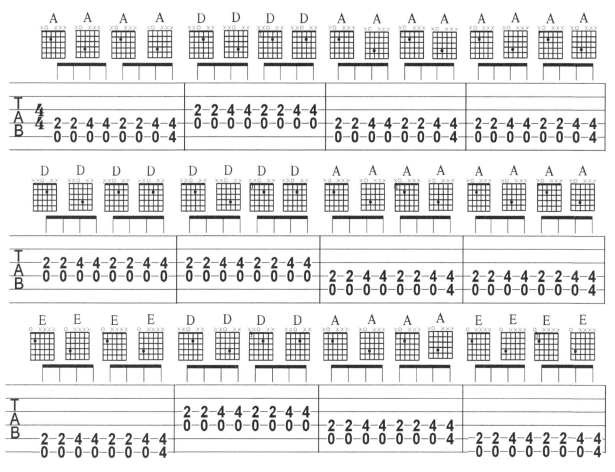

You can play this vamp pattern on chords in any key. To play this vamp on chords that don't use open bass strings, like E, A and D, you can use a two note power chord (pg.17) to execute the pattern. The only trick is that you need to identify the note under your 1st finger to determine the name of the chord. See the fingerboard chart on pg. 36 for a complete fingerboard chart.

If you are playing a blues in the key of E, the 1, 4 and 5 chords will be E, A and B. You will need to find a B power chord, and play the vamp in that position. B is the note on the 2nd fret of the 5th string, so place the power chord there, and follow the TAB on the right. You can use power chords with the root on the 5th or 6th string to play this vamp up the neck.

B Power Chord
(root on the A string)

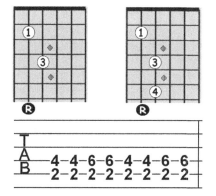

How to Jam

The scale shown here is the E minor pentatonic scale, which is a very useful scale for jamming. It can be played over songs in the key of E, especially blues and rock tunes. The scale is shown in TAB, as well as with the diagram on the right. The numbers represent left hand fingering. O means open string.

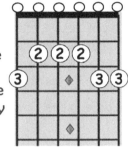

Play the scale, one note at a time, first using down strokes with the pick. Try using rest strokes as you learn this scale. As you play each note, have the pick come to rest on the adjacent string. This will help make each note ring out clearly. When you are comfortable with the scale, start playing alternating down– up pick strokes. This will help you develop speed. Make sure that you hold each note down with your left hand until you are ready to play the next note. You don't want any dead air in between the notes.

E Minor Pentatonic Scale

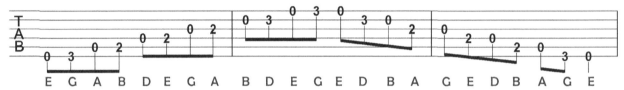

Extending the Minor Pentatonic Scale

Below is a slightly extended version of the E minor pentatonic scale. This shape gives you a few more notes to play in the scale, as well as getting you to start playing up the neck. All of the techniques presented in this section can be used with this extended fingering, including the additional notes in the blues scale.

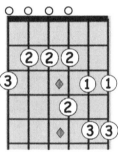

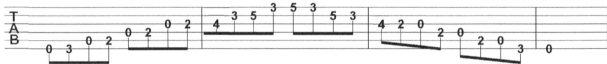

How to Use The Minor Pentatonic Scale

Earlier in this book the major scale was introduced. The major scale has seven notes (or degrees). Starting from the root (which is 1), they are: R 2 3 4 5 6 7.

If you took a major scale and only played the root, lowered the third note by a half step, the fourth, the fifth, and lowered the seventh note by a half step, you would get a minor pentatonic scale. The minor pentatonic scale has only five notes. They are R b3 4 5 b7.

The great utility of the minor pentatonic scale, and why it is used extensively by lead guitarists of all stripes, is that when played over many tunes, especially blues, it contains no dissonance. That is, you can play virtually any note from the scale and insert it anywhere in the tune, and it will sound musical.

There are three techniques you can incorporate when using any scale for soloing. They are: *playing licks, playing like a singer,* and *playing chord tones.* The next couple of pages will elaborate on these techniques.

The best way to apply soloing techniques is to have another guitarist to jam with. One guitarist plays the chords, and the other solos. If you don't have a playing partner, you can record yourself playing the chords, and jam over them. There are also lots of apps and programs, like Band in a Box, that can generate play along tracks.

Playing Licks

A lick is a musical phrase that can be played over a given chord, or chord sequence. Licks are what many lead guitarists use when they play a solo.

There are thousands of licks that you can find in books, on line, listening to tunes, or just coming up with them yourself. You can get a lot of mileage out of licks, and can play some compelling solos by drawing from your vocabulary of licks. You can play many minor pentatonic licks over virtually every chord in a blues, without changing the lick.

Below are minor pentatonic licks in the key of E that can be played over a 12 bar blues in E. You can also sequence them to create longer lines. Observe the timing for each lick.

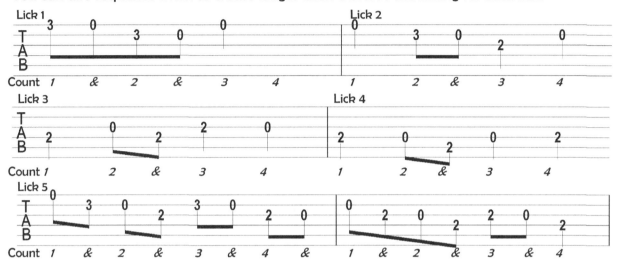

Playing Like a Singer

Playing a solo with a lot of notes can be pretty liberating, but many of the great solos are more like mini musical compositions, not just displays of technical prowess. Sometimes a guitar solo jumps right out of the song, and while it may be an amazing piece of shredding, it may not feel like a part of the song.

Play like a singer. Make your solo an instrumental extension of what a vocalist would be doing. That means try to create melodies as you play. Keep in mind that the silence between notes can be just as powerful as the notes played. You can use the other techniques from this chapter—licks, chord tones, but always try to play with taste. You can let your solo build to a flashy climax, but while you're getting there, try to play like a singer.

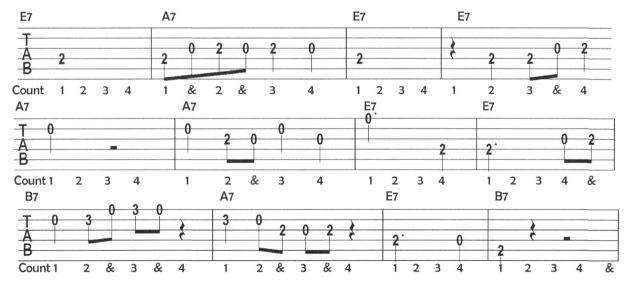

Playing Chord Tones

When you play a solo, the listener should be able to discern the form of the song under your solo. That is, the notes in your solo should reflect the chord that it is being played over. Being able to identify, and play notes from the underlying chord (chord tones), will give your solo a lot more depth and musicality.

A typical blues tune contains the 1^7, 4^7, and 5^7 chords. The blues in the key of E would include E^7, A^7, and B^7. The notes in an E minor pentatonic scale are E G A B, and D, and since the E minor pentatonic scale contains an E, an A, and a B note, that means it contains the root notes for the 1, 4, and 5 chords in the blues chord progression in the key of E.
If you play over the chords in the progression, and play the root note of each chord, your solo will be aligned with the chords. However, just playing the root note of each chord would be a bit simplistic, and boring, so, if you play the root note of each chord as it spins by, and add other notes from the scale, your solo will gain power.

Below is the E minor pentatonic scale displayed by note names, and scale degrees. You can see the R, 4, and 5 notes (E, A and B), so when an E ^{7}(1) chord is being played, play a lick that emphasizes the E note (R). When an A^7 chord (4 chord) is being played, play an A note (4), and so on. The licks on this page use this approach to developing motifs, and will show some specific licks that can be played over each chord.

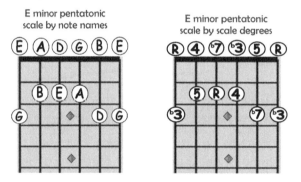

The example below shows a 12 bar blues in E, with a solo using the E minor pentatonic scale. Each measure (except measure 12) starts with a note in the scale that matches the chord in that measure. Motifs are developed from that note, but playing the root of the chord in-stantly connects the solo with the chords. You can even "hear" the chord progression when you play the solo unaccompanied.

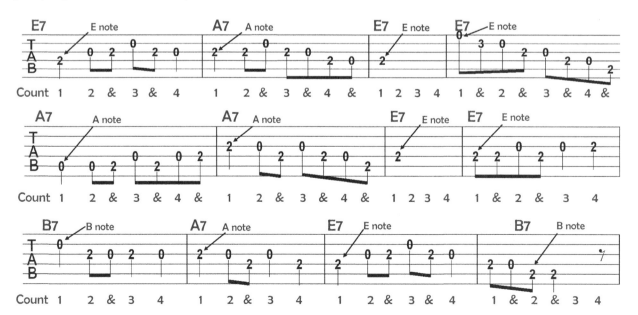

The Moveable Minor Pentatonic Scale

Just as open chords can be adjusted to become moveable chords, open scales can be refingered, and played up the neck in any key. The minor pentatonic scale is shown here as a moveable scale, making it easy to navigate through different keys.

The root of the scale is indicated by the black notes, and if you can identify the root on the 6th string, 4th or 1st string, you can find this scale in any key. Just as there are five major scale forms that conform with CAGED system, there are five pentatonic forms. This form is the E form. The four other forms will be introduced on pg. 66.

The TAB below shows the minor pentatonic (blues) scale in the key of A. The A note is the root of the scale, and resides on the 5th fret of the 6th string. You can play this scale in any key. i.e. If the song is in the key of C, find the C note on the 6th string (8th fret) and start the scale from that point.

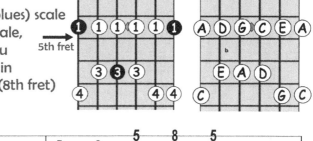

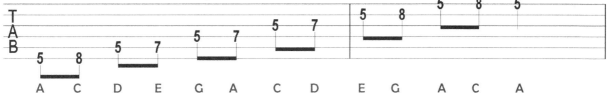

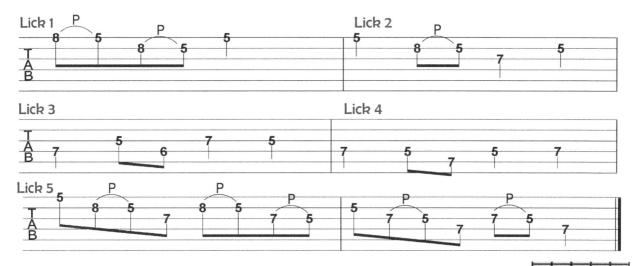

Extending the Moveable Minor Pentatonic Scale

Just as with the E minor pentatonic scale, you can extend the moveable version. With the moveable scale you can also extend to some notes that are lower than the root. Here is the same A minor pentatonic scale, as above, but with extensions on the top and bottom of the scale.

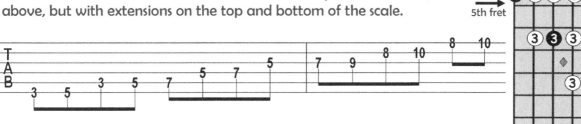

The Blues Scale

You can add one note to the minor pentatonic scale and add a lot of color to your solos. This is called the blues scale. The diagrams and TAB show the E minor blues scale. The blues scale is created by adding a note between the fourth and fifth degree of the scale, making it a b (flatted) fifth degree (or # fourth).

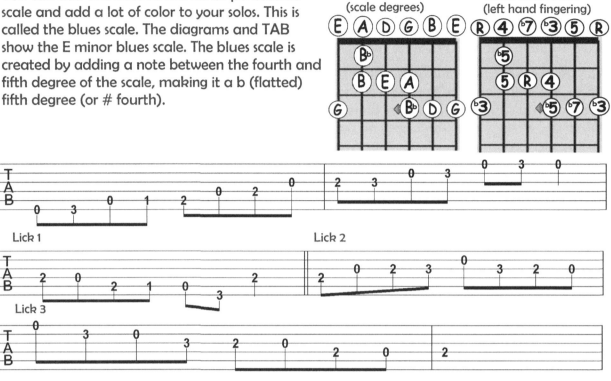

The Moveable Blues Scale

Use the same method that you use to move the minor pentatonic scale up and down the neck for the blues scale. Simply identify the root, and play!

Below are the same licks as above in a moveable form using the A minor blues scale.

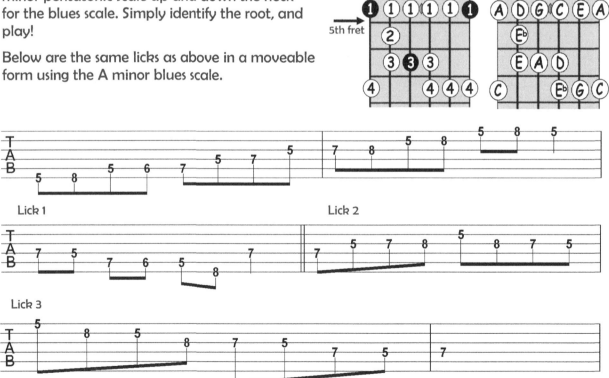

The Major Pentatonic Scale

While the minor pentatonic scale is ideal for playing blues and rock solos, the major pentatonic scale is a great vehicle for playing solos over country and bluegrass tunes. It looks a lot like the minor pentatonic scale, but observe where the root resides in the diagrams below.

Just as the minor pentatonic is "extracted" from the major scale, the major pentatonic scale is constructed from the R, 2nd, 3rd, 5th, and 6th degrees of the major scale. The scale displayed here is the G major pentatonic and the extended major pentatonic scale.

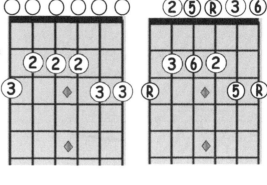

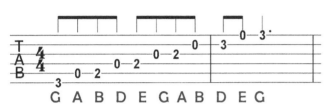

Here are a series of major pentatonic licks over a G, D, Em, C chord sequence. Remember, even though the G major pentatonic looks like the E minor pentatonic, its application is over chords in the key of G, not E.

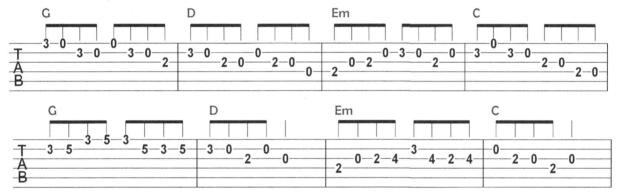

Extended Major Pentatonic Scale

Here is an extended version of the major pentatonic scale. Like the minor pentatonic scale, this little extension gives you several more notes to play out of the basic scale.

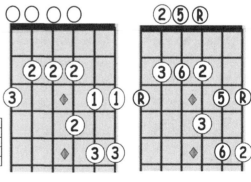

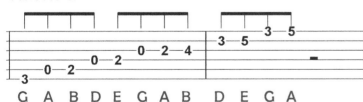

Here is a lick using the extended G major pentatonic scale.

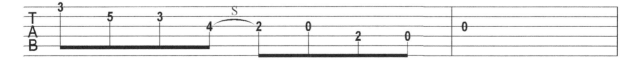

The Moveable Major Pentatonic Scale

Just as the minor pentatonic and blues scale can be played up the neck, the major pentatonic (and major blues scale) can be played anywhere and in any key.

The A major pentatonic scale shown here looks a lot like its minor counterpart, but observe where the root resides. (black numbers) Playing this sequence of notes from different root positions is what allows the same sequence of notes to have a completely different sound.

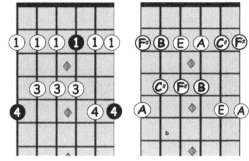

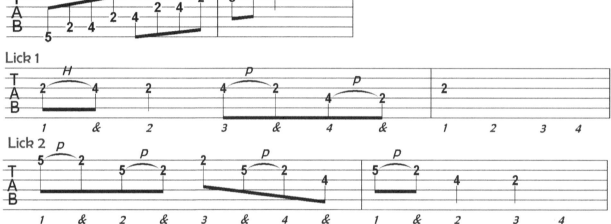

Lick 1

Lick 2

Lick 3 This one extends slightly out of the scale shape.

The Major Blues Scale

You can create a blues scale with a major pentatonic by adding a note in between 2nd and 3rd degrees of the scale. The scale and licks displayed use the A major blues scale.

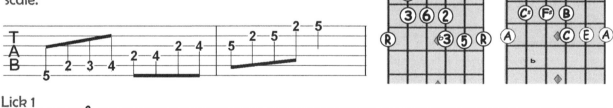

Lick 1

Lick 2

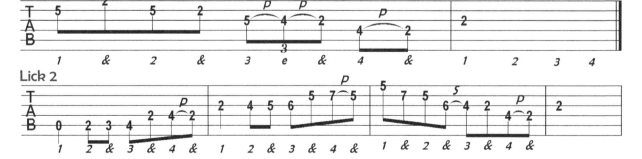

The Sliding Pentatonic Scales

The Sliding Minor Pentatonic Scale

A very effective way to play the minor pentatonic scale is with the sliding scale, which enables you to travel up and down the neck easily, and add more note choices for your solos.

There are two sliding scale shapes—one that has the root on the 6th string, and one that has the root on the 5th string. The diagrams on the right show the left hand fingering for these scales, with the root shown in black.

You only need to use your 1st and 3rd finger to execute this scale, and you can slide from one note to another where indicated by an Ⓢ.

Below is the sliding minor pentatonic scale in G.

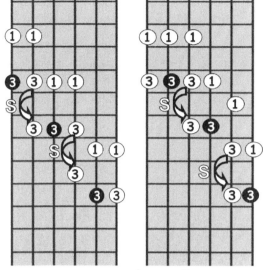

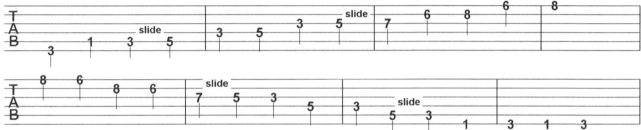

The Sliding Major Pentatonic Scale

The major pentatonic scale can also be played as a sliding scale. Just identify the root, notated with a black dot, and you will be able to play this scale over any chord, in any key.

You can use the major pentatonic scale to play over all of the chords in a song, but you can also shift the scale through the song, and play a different pentatonic scale over each major chord.

If a song starts with a G chord, use a major pentatonic scale starting on a G note. If a C chord appears, start a new scale with C as the root, and so on.

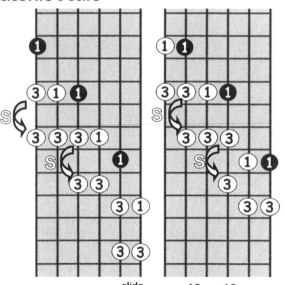

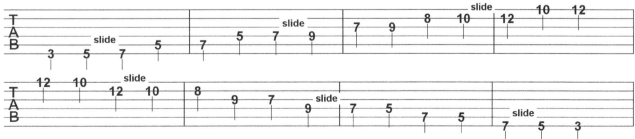

The Rest of the Pentatonic Scales

Below are all five major and minor pentatonic scales. They are organized just as the five moveable chord shapes are, using the CAGED system, and displayed by scale degree. The black B indicates the note that you can add to any pentatonic scale to make it a blues scale.

You should try to include as many of these scale patterns in your vocabulary as you can, and try to learn the same licks in each one. This will help you develop a command of the fingerboard by being able to play the same idea anywhere on the neck. You should also start looking at other scales that will expand your melodic potential. As you progress, you should learn all of the major, and minor scale patterns, as presented in my book, *Fear of Soloing.*

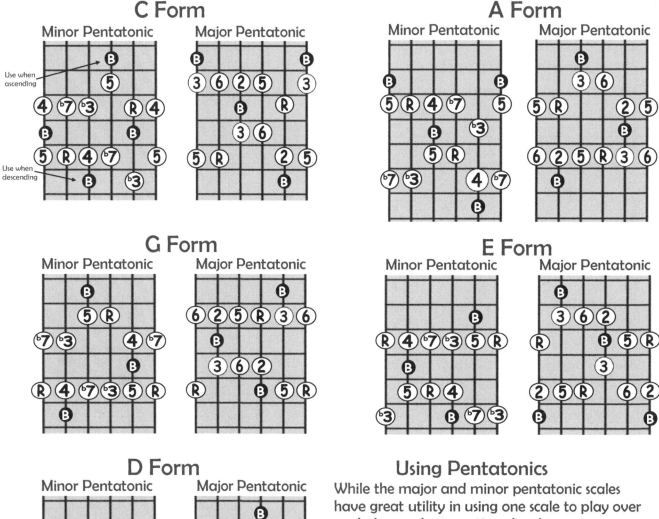

Using Pentatonics

While the major and minor pentatonic scales have great utility in using one scale to play over a whole song by targeting chord tones, a more enlightened approach is to shift the scales you are using to the chord being played.

If a song moves from an A chord to a D chord, use an A pentatonic scale over the A chord and a D pentatonic scale over the D chord. This will give you more notes to choose to play over any given chord.

Pentatonic Tricks

There is a very useful trick that you can employ with the pentatonic scales. If you play a minor pentatonic scale anywhere on the neck, you can slide the scale down three frets and the same fingering will become a major pentatonic scale in the same key and, if you play a major pentatonic scale, you can slide it up three frets, and it will become a minor pentatonic scale.

This trick will enable you to slide seamlessly between major and minor pentatonic scales, and toggle your solo between a bluesy or a country type of sound. The examples below illustrate this technique.

Ex 1. This lick starts with a minor pentatonic lick on the 5th fret (A minor pentatonic). The lick is slid down three frets, and exact pattern is repeated. Now, however it is a major pentatonic lick (A major pentatonic). Notice that while the pattern is the same, the root note is in a different place in the two scales.

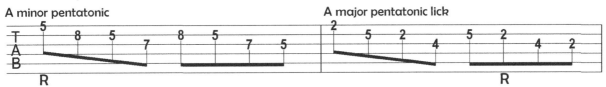

Ex 2. This lick starts with an A major pentatonic lick on the 5th fret. The lick is slid up three frets, and becomes an A minor pentatonic lick. Once again, observe where the root resides in each scale lick. You can do this with any pentatonic lick!

Bending Notes

Bending notes is technique that is used extensively when playing pentatonic scales.

To bend a note hold a note down with your third finger, with your first and second finger supporting it.

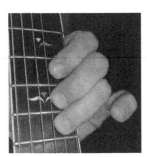

Pick the note, and push it across the fingerboard until it's a whole step higher.

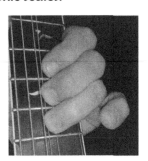

While you can bend any note that you choose, the most recognizable bendable notes reside on the fourth and flatted seventh degrees in the minor pentatonic scale, and the second and sixth degrees of the major pentatonic scale.

The next page will present some typical bending licks for the major and minor pentatonic scale. Be aware that it's much easier to bend strings on an electric guitar, especially when you are bending the third string. But, you can still get pretty slinky on an acoustic.

Bending Licks

Here is a basic bend and bend release. Put your third finger on the seventh fret of the second string, with you first and second finger supporting it, and push all three up a whole step.

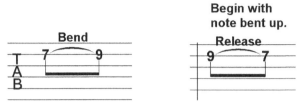

Here is a basic bend and bend release lick. This is a major pentatonic lick in E.

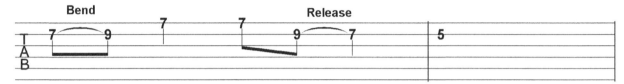

Here is a variation of the above. Leave your pinky on the seventh fret of the first string while executing the bend and release.

This lick bends the third string. Bar the pad of your fourth finger across the first two strings at the twelfth fret.

Here are a couple of minor pentatonic licks. Remember, move these licks down three frets, and they become major pentatonic licks.

Key of A   Key of G

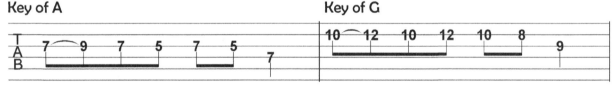

This lick bends the third string from the seventh fret up a whole step. Bar the pad of your first finger across the first two strings at the fifth fret.

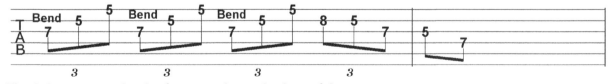

This lick starts on the & of one, and is in the key of A.

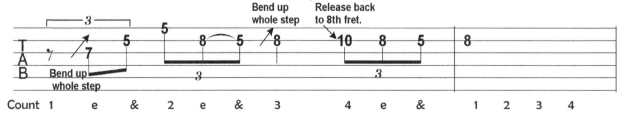

Pentatonic Studies

The next two pages include two solos that apply all of the techniques presented in this section. The first is a solo over a 12 bar blues that uses the moveable minor pentatonic scale in the key of A, and resides within the E form, with the extended notes on the first three strings.

Locate the A minor pentatonic scale by finding the A note (root) on the sixth string, and playing the moveable minor pentatonic scale from there.

Minor Pentatonic Study

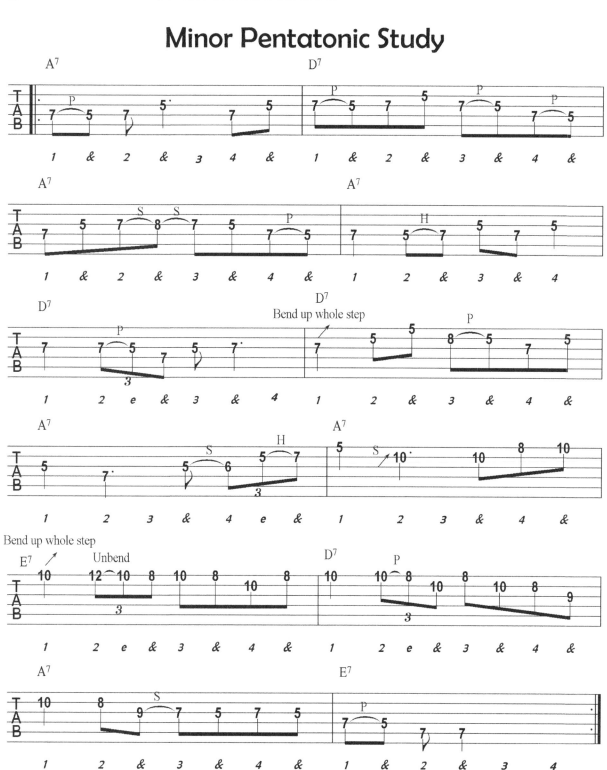

This solo focuses on the major pentatonic scale. Remember that any major or minor pentatonic lick can be moved up or down three frets to convert from major to minor, or minor to major.

Major Pentatonic Study

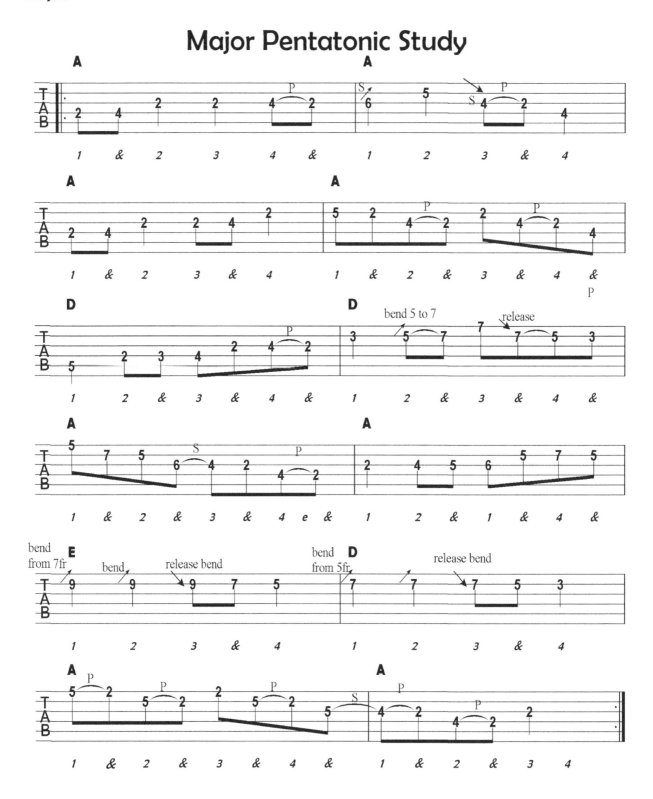

Soloing with the Major Scale

The major scale was introduced earlier as a tool for understanding chords, but here we will take a look at the major scale as a soloing device. You have to be a bit more selective in using the major scale in a solo, as opposed to the pentatonic scale, but it does offer a huge range of soloing ideas when you know which notes work over different chords.

The major scale is the familiar sounding *do re mi fa sol la ti do,* and can be generated from any note. The formula for the major scale is a sequence of whole and half steps. A half step is the distance from one fret to the next fret up or down. A whole step is the distance between two frets. The formula in whole and half steps for a major scale is:

whole whole half whole whole whole half

Using this formula, a G major scale would look like this:
G (w) A (w) B (1/2) C (w) D (w) E (w) F# (1/2) G
Below, for clarity, is the scale shown on a piano keyboard.

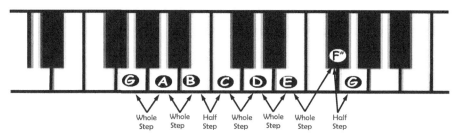

Here is the major scale on the guitar fingerboard, starting from the open G string, using the W W 1/2 W W W 1/2 formula.

Notice that in following the major scale formula the we had to include the F# note to create the Do Re Mi Fa Sol La Ti Do sound .

Every key except the key of C employs a certain number of accidentals (sharps or flats) to comply with the major scale formula. Only the C scale contains only natural notes and no accidentals.

You can see that the G scale that we have produced requires a lot of movement up and down the neck. This is a graphic representation of the scale. The next few pages will put this scale into a more manageable finger pattern that can be used to create an infinite number of melodies.

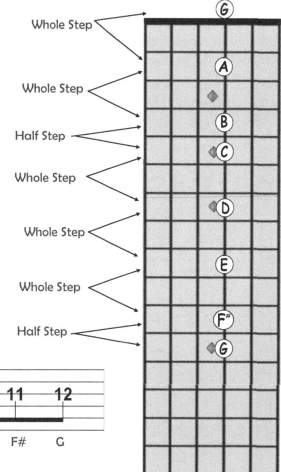

```
T
A   0   2   4   5   7   9   11  12
B

    G   A   B   C   D   E   F#  G
```

Now that we have established the notes in the G scale, we can place them in a more logical pattern, rather than playing each scale vertically up the fingerboard on one string.

The G major scale is notated below by note name, left hand fingering, and scale degree.

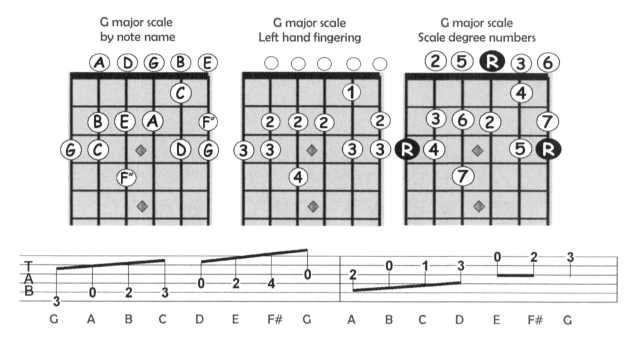

Below is a repeating pattern using the open G scale. It's a great way to get your hands warmed up. Try to use alternating strokes with your pick: down-up-down-up

You can apply this pattern to any open or moveable scale. It is a great exercise, but it is also great ammunition for creating solos.

Here is the G scale as a moveable form, also displayed by note name, left hand fingering, and scale degree. This is the E form moveable scale, and explained earlier, is the motor behind the E form moveable chords.

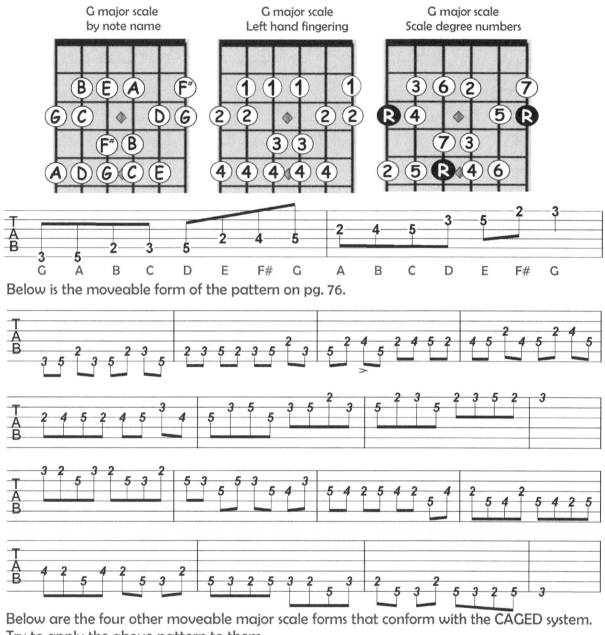

Below is the moveable form of the pattern on pg. 76.

Below are the four other moveable major scale forms that conform with the CAGED system. Try to apply the above pattern to them.

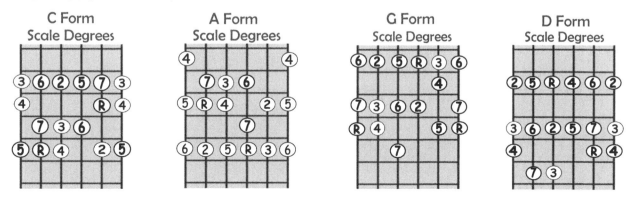

Targeting Chord Tones

You can employ the same chord tone technique that we used with the pentatonic scale when playing a major scale over a chord sequence. Below is a G D Em C chord sequence, and each measure begins with the root of the chord played in that measure, using just the notes of a G major scale. The first three examples use the open G scale.

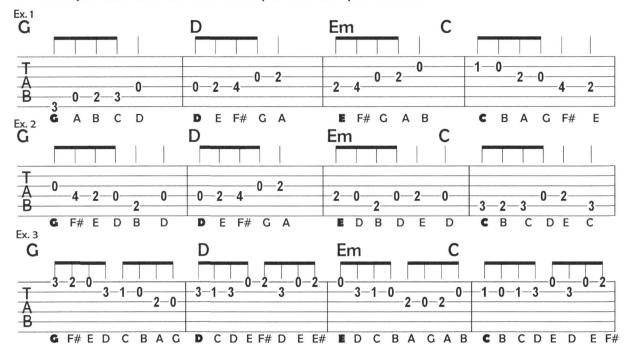

Below are the same examples as above, but they are notated using the moveable G scale. The same notes are played, put they are all on fretted notes, not open strings. Once you can play melodies using the moveable scale, you can play melodies anywhere on the neck, and in any key.

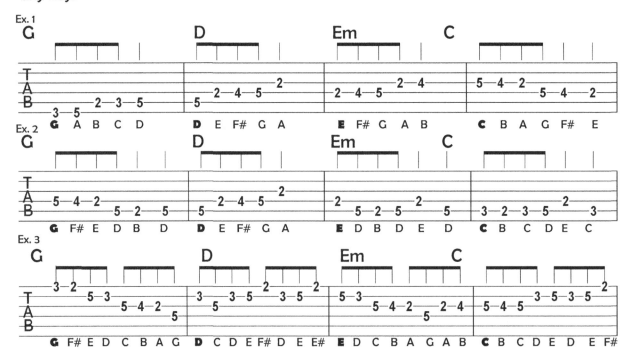

Soloing with the Minor Scale

Now that we have introduced scales as a vehicle for playing melodies, and improvising, you should start looking at some of the other scales so you can play melodically over any chord sequence. There are many scales that you should learn, but there are three scales that will serve you well in virtually any melodic situation—the major scale, the pentatonic scale, and the minor scale.

There are several minor scales that you will encounter, but the one presented here has the most utility. It's called the dorian mode, and it is a scale that is extracted from a major scale. If you played the notes in a G scale starting and ending on an A note, you would be playing the A dorian mode. There are modes that are built from every note in the major scale, and these too will be an area to focus on as you develop as a guitarist.

The dorian scale is like a major scale with the third and seventh degree lowered a half step. The dorian mode can be played in five shapes, just like the major scale. The scales below are arranged in he same manner as the CAGED system. The black note indicates the root.

The Dorian Mode

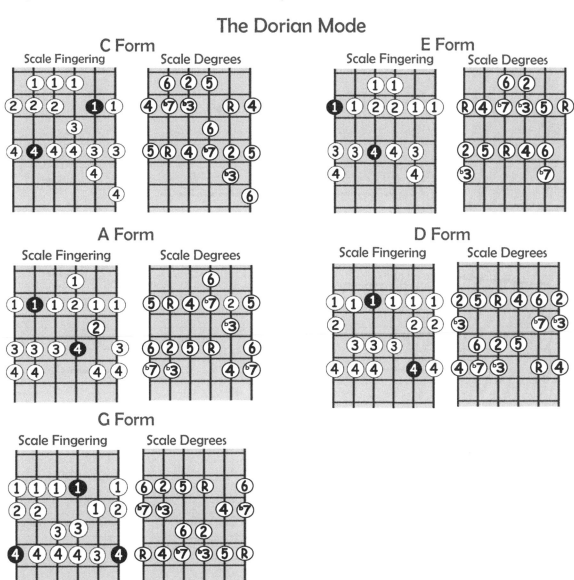

Below is a study that employs the dorian mode over a 12 bar minor blues. A minor blues is a 12 blues bar form, but the 1 and 4 chord are minor. The 5 chord is typically a 7th chord.

In this study, the A dorian is used over the A minor chords, and the D dorian is used over the D minor chords. The last two bars use the A minor blues scale over the A minor and E7 chords.

You will find that the dorian mode, the minor pentatonic scale, and the blues scale work well together, and are somewhat interchangeable.

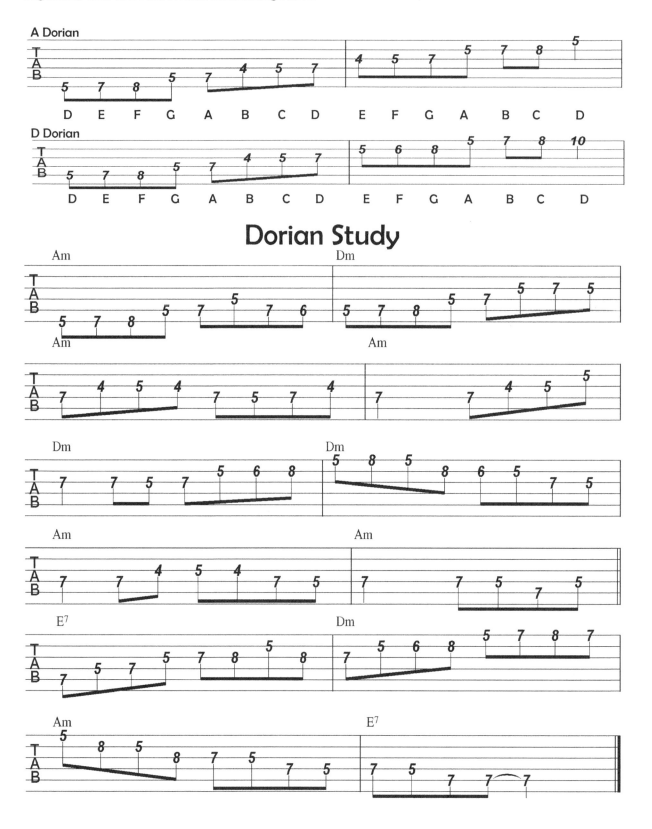

Dorian Study

Beyond Chord Tones

While using the notes in a scale to create melodies is an important tool for improvising, it starts to get real interesting when you start inserting notes that are not in the scale to create tension and resolution in your solos. You also can start using a variety of scales to play over different chords. For instance, playing a major pentatonic scale over a major chord, a Dorian scale over a minor chord, etc. The examples on this page will explore this concept. You are only limited by your own creativity. If it sounds good, it's music!

The first example uses a fragment of a scale over each chord, and adds a chromatic note in between notes of the scale. Chromatic means playing successive half steps—not adhering to any particular scale. The example also shifts the melody to a scale that corresponds to each chord: G scale for G, D scale for D, E dorian for Em, and C major for C.

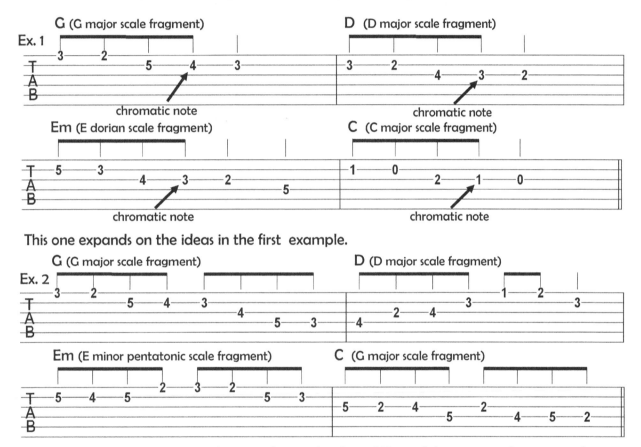

This one expands on the ideas in the first example.

Here the minor pentatonic scale is used over the G and Em, while major scales are used over the D and C chords.

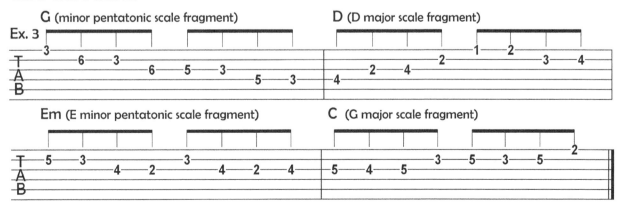

Bluegrass Licks and Soloing

Bluegrass picking, or flatpicking, is a challenging and exciting way to play the guitar. It requires strong right hand picking technique, and this lesson will provide you with the tools needed to play licks and solos over many bluegrass tunes. You should seek out some fiddle tunes to help build your technique in this style. (Salt Creek, Bill Cheatham, Whiskey Before Breakfast, Big Sciota, Billy in the Low Ground, etc).

Three major scales (G, C and D), and one minor scale (E aeolian) will be used. You need to learn these scales, and the licks that are presented with each scale, as they will give you some ammunition to play solos over any bluegrass tune. Each scale starts on the root and is played to the first string, then descends back to the root, and continues to the notes in the scale that are below the root.

Bluegrass relies heavily on the major scale, but the major and minor pentatonic scales should also be part of your vocabulary for playing bluegrass solos.

As you play through each scale, try to use alternating pick strokes- down-up-down-up.

 The "S" connecting some notes indicates a slide. Play the note before the S, and slide into the next note. The "P" indicates a pull off. Play the note before the P then snap your finger back to produce the sound of the next note. Don't play the note with your pick. The pull off should be executed entirely by your left hand. On pages 85 and 86 there are a couple of flatpicking solos that employ the licks and scales presented in this lesson.

Key of G—Scale and Licks

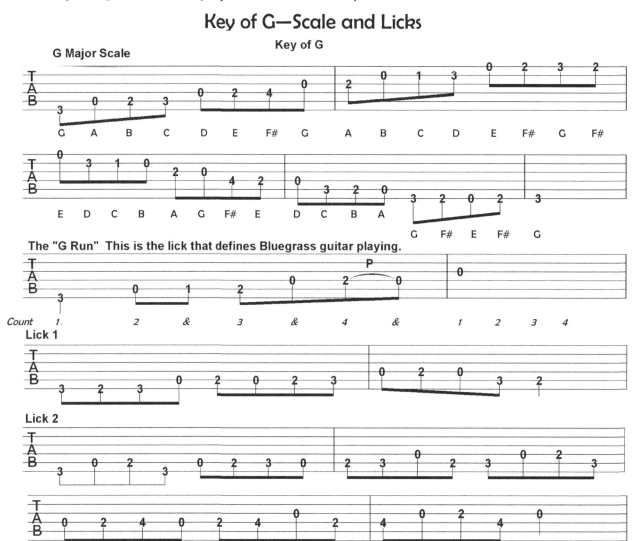

Lick 3

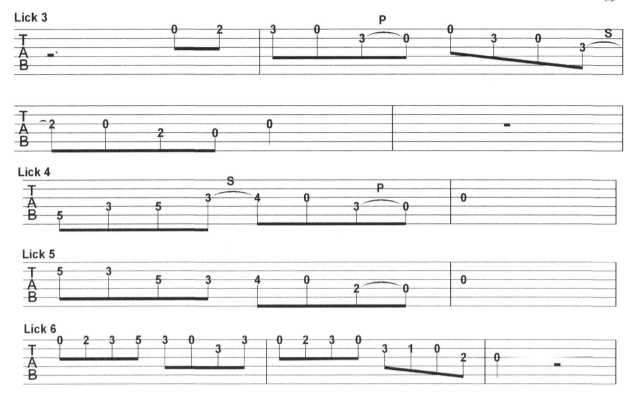

The next two licks are in the style of Tony Rice, and have a very bluesy quality. They employ the minor pentatonic scale, as well as a couple of notes not included in the scale. While the major and pentatonic scales are the motor that drives this style, you are not relegated to playing just the notes in the scale. You can use a scale as a basis for a solo, and add notes outside the scale as you see fit.

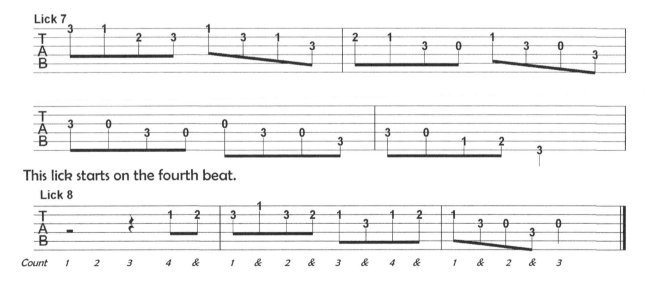

This lick starts on the fourth beat.

Key of C—Scale and Licks

Here is the C scale with several licks that you can use to play over a C chord.

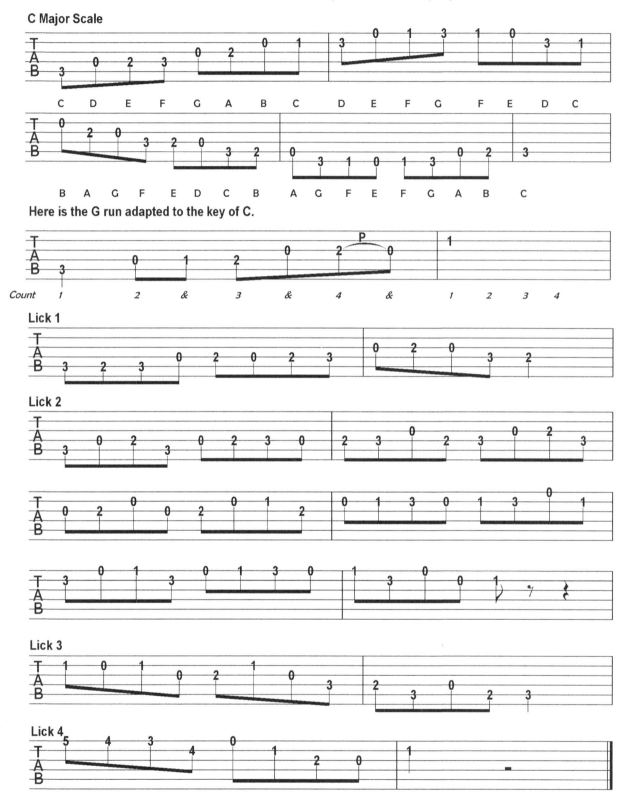

C Major Scale

Here is the G run adapted to the key of C.

Lick 1

Lick 2

Lick 3

Lick 4

Key of D—Scale and Licks

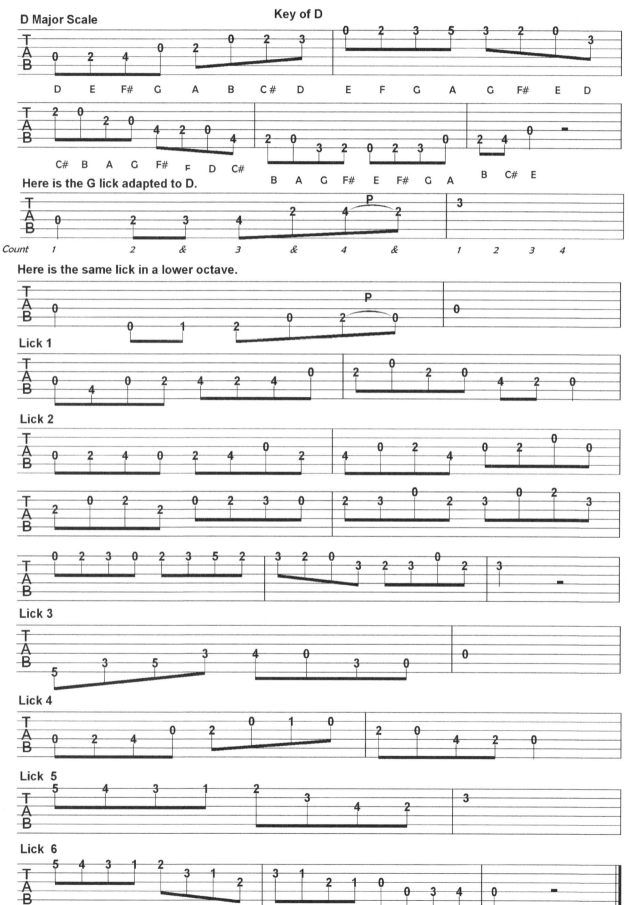

Key of Em—Scale and Licks

Lots of bluegrass/country tunes contain minor chords, so we'll add some licks that will work with them. The scale presented here is a minor scale called the aeolian mode. Like the dorian mode introduced earlier, the aeolian mode is a scale that is extracted from a major scale. If you start a major scale on the sixth degree, and play the scale to the sixth degree an octave higher, you get the aeolian mode. The actual scale degrees from the root of the aeolian mode are R 2 b3 4 5 b6 b7.

The E aeolian mode is used here since the Em is a typical chord in the key of G, and will conform to the other scales and licks in this lesson.

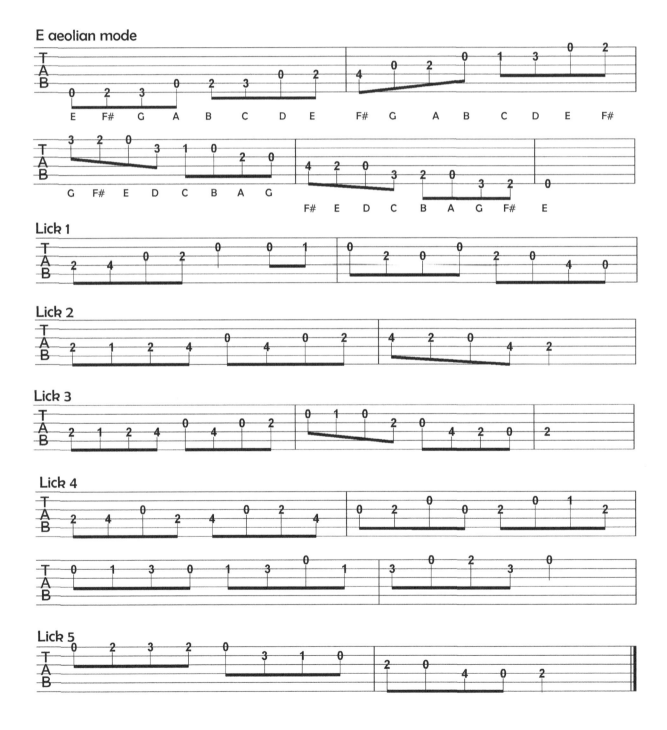

Bluegrass Study 1

The following solo follows the chord progression for Bill Cheatham, a popular bluegrass fiddle tune. It is comprised almost entirely of G, C, and D licks from the last few pages. As you add more licks to your vocabulary, you can craft solos by inserting them over the chords in a tune.

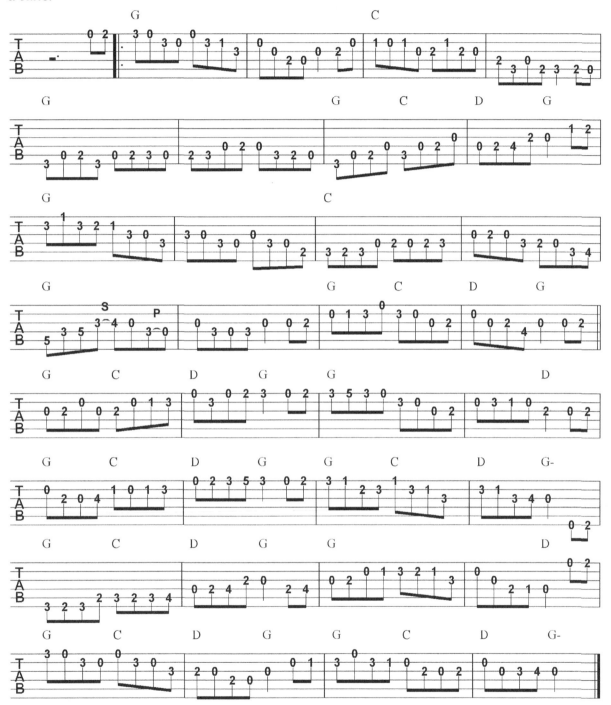

Bluegrass Study 2

Here is another flatpicking solo set to the chord changes of the fiddle tune, Big Sciota. This tune has an Em chord in it, and the E aeolian mode is used.

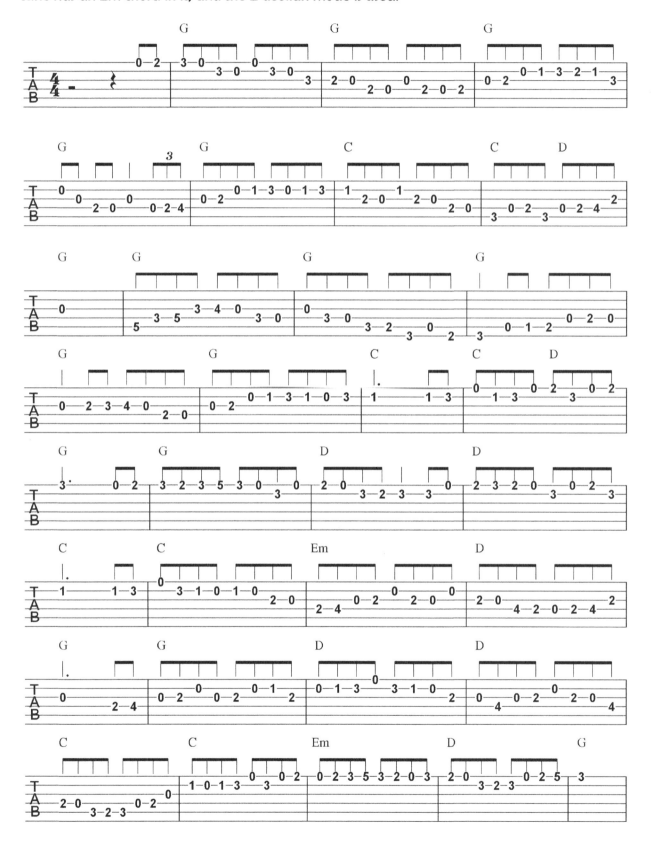

Fingerstyle Guitar

Playing guitar "fingerstyle" opens a whole world of possibilities for accompanying songs, and playing solo arrangements. In fingerstyle playing, you approach the guitar like a piano. Just as on a piano, where your left hand plays the bass notes, and your right hand plays the melody, on guitar, your thumb plays the bass notes, and your fingers play the melody notes.

The first example shows, what is called, an arpeggio pattern. Your thumb plays the first note, index finger the second note, middle finger, the third note, and ring finger plays the fourth note. There are countless variations of this pattern. You can use only your thumb, index and middle fingers, and you can play the pattern over any of the notes that are included in the chord.

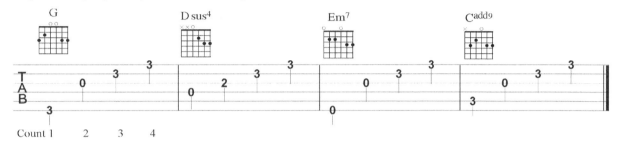

Here is the same pattern, with two notes on each beat. Use a repeating right hand pattern of thumb, index, middle, ring, thumb, index, middle, ring.

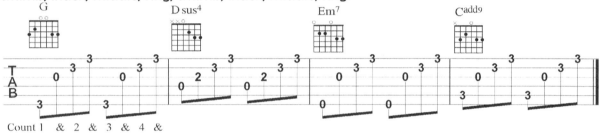

Here is the same pattern with your middle and ring fingers plucking two strings at once on the 2nd, 3rd, and 4th beats.

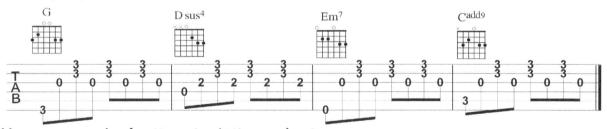

Here are a couple of patterns in 3/4 time—3 beats per measure.

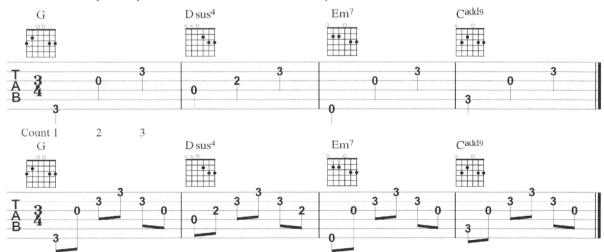

Travis Picking

There are many ways to play the guitar with you fingers instead of a pick, but the most popular approach is the alternating thumb style, often referred to as Travis style, after the fingerstyle pioneer, Merle Travis.

Travis style, also known as Chet Atkins style, Delta blues and Piedmont blues styles, incorporates a steady alternating bass pattern, played on the bass strings with your thumb, while your fingers play a repeating melodic pattern on the treble strings. The pattern is similar to the alternating bass note/strum of the country strum.

Here is a 1, 4, 5 chord sequence in the key of G. The alternating bass notes are played on each beat with your thumb. A metronome can come in handy while learning this style. Play it slowly until it becomes effortless.

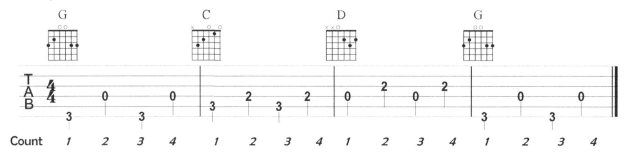

The next step is to add melody notes. You can insert melody notes on any beat, or the "and" of any beat. This gives you eight possible rhythmic locations for the melody notes.

The melody notes and the bass notes do not generally share strings. So, if you are playing a G chord, the bass notes would own the 4th, 5th and 6th strings, and the melody notes would be relegated to the 1st, 2nd and 3rd strings.

We'll start with a melody note on the first beat. This melody note is pinched on the first beat with your thumb playing the bass note.

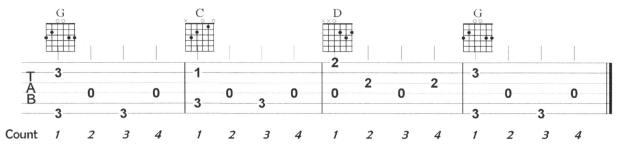

Now, you add a melody note on the & of the second beat. This note is played in between the bass notes on the 2nd and 3rd beats. Make sure that the alternating bass pattern doesn't get interrupted when you insert the melody notes.

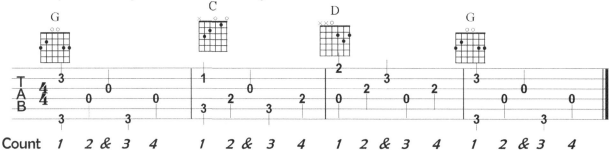

Watch a video of this lesson at
www.nofearbooks.com

You can add melody notes wherever you want. Here is the first pattern with an additional melody note played on the "&" of the third beat.

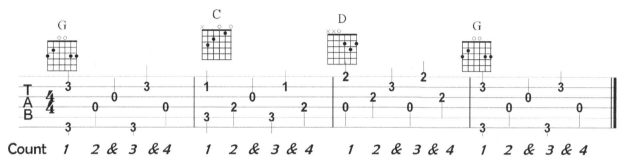

Fingerstyle Study

Below is a 12 bar blues played fingerstyle. Remember, you can use any combination of melody notes on the count, or the & of the count. Experiment!

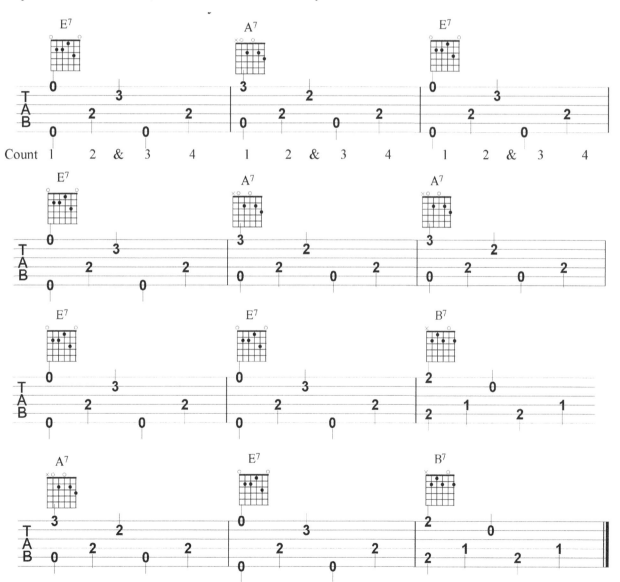

Adding Chords to Patterns

You can get a lot of mileage out of these fingerstyle patterns by adding different versions of the same chord with your left hand. If you know several different versions of the same chord, you can insert them into the tune, while playing the same right hand pattern. It will add a lot of variety to the tune.

Below are four 7th chords that can be substituted for the standard chords. The root of each chord is notated, so to play the chord in a given key, just find the root note on the appropriate string.

The following example is the same 12 bar blues as before, but we have inserted these new chord "voicings" to add more color. Notice that while the chords are only fretted on four strings, you can play the open E and A string with your thumb to complete the alternating thumb pattern.

Alternate 7th chords

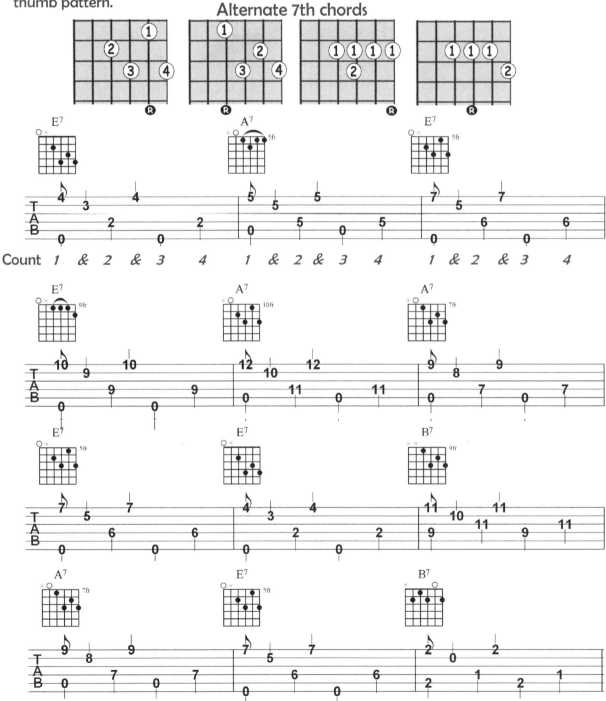

Adding Melody Notes

Once you are comfortable with playing these fingerstyle patterns, you can start inserting melodies. Instead of playing a repeating pattern with your right hand, you can play melodies that can change from measure to measure. This can be a bit tricky at first because when you play melodies, you are breaking away from the comfort zone of the repeating pattern, and making your fingers become completely independent, rhythmically, from your thumb. Your left hand also will have to shift from the original chord fingering to accommodate melody notes.

The following example is a 12 bar blues that uses the same melody for each measure, but observe that to execute the melody notes, your left hand has to add notes for each chord. Your pinky has to add a note on the second string for the E and B7 chords, and your ring finger has to lift up to get the melody note on the second string.

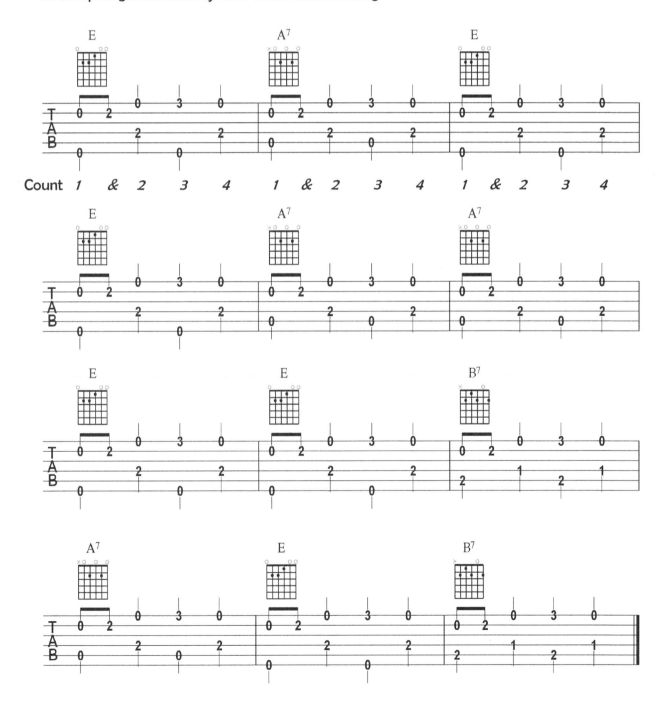

More Melody Notes

The example below is another 12 bar blues that uses melodic phrases instead of a repeating pattern. In this example the melody is a bit more sophisticated in that the melody phrase is different in each measure. Many of the melody choices are from the minor pentatonic scale. When you add melody notes you can add notes from the pentatonic, major, or minor scales depending on the type of chord you are playing, but feel free to just grab random notes that are in the vicinity of the chord and see if they work.

Observe that in measures 3, 7, and 10 a melody note is played on the & of the fourth beat, and is tied to the first beat of the next measure. That means that the tied note on the first beat is not played—it just keeps ringing from the note played on the & of four. This can be a little tricky, so count and play slowly until it's fluid. Make sure that your thumb keeps the alternating pattern on each beat.

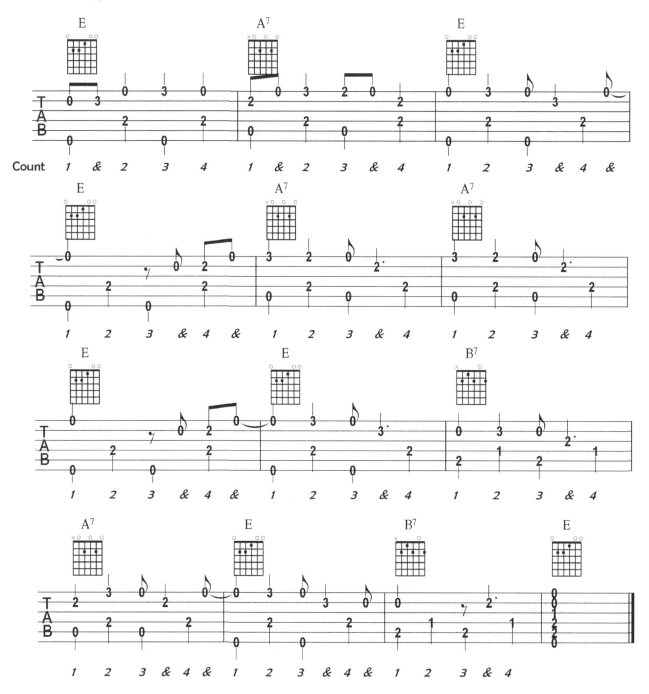

Alternate Chords with Melody

Alternate Chords with Melody

Here we put all of the previous techniques together. This is a 12 bar blues using alternate chords, and adding melody phrases throughout. The trick here is to be able to reach outside the chord to grab melody notes. Two of the alternate 7th chords presented earlier are shown here. You will have to bar across a few strings with your index finger to accommodate the melody notes that are played with these chords.

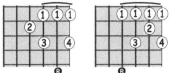

All of the E and A chords in this example can be played using the fifth and sixth string as a bass note. In measure nine you can see a B7 chord with one of the alternate chord voicings. While there is no open string for the bass note, you can move the alternating bass to the third and fourth string to maintain the alternating bass pattern, leaving the first two strings for the melody.

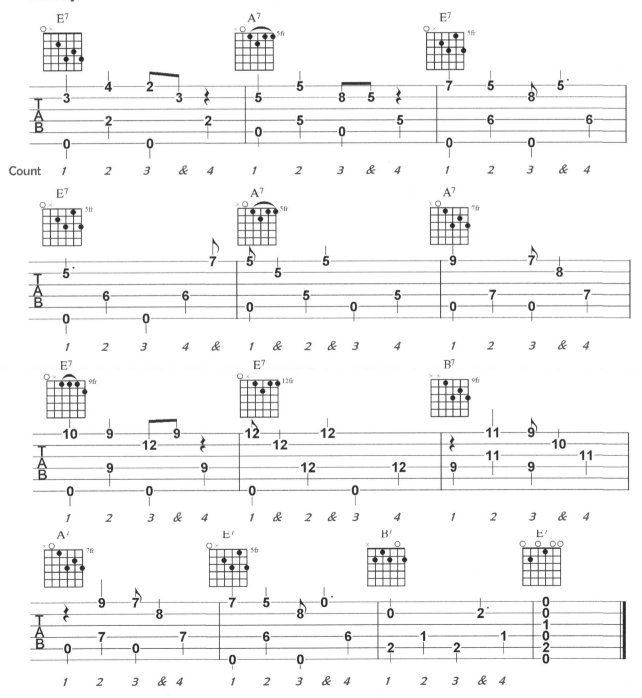

More on Chord Families

Now that we have established that you can add scale degrees to a chord, and give it more character, (i.e. Cadd9, Gm7) you should look at some of the other "extended" chords that you will encounter in songs. The chart below shows the most common chord extensions that occur in each chord family. You can see that each extended chord still contains the basic components of the chord (R 3 5 etc.), but has added other notes from the associated scale.

The value in knowing the different chords that populate each chord family is that it enables you to insert different chords in a song where a basic chord is called for. All of the chords in each chord family are basically interchangeable, and can be substituted and added to standard chord progressions. You do have to be somewhat selective stylistically, however. You won't want to insert a 7#5 chord in a bluegrass tune, but an add9 might be appropriate. Having this understanding of chords will increase your chord vocabulary, and enable you to add lots of color to any tune.

Major Family

Basic major chord	R 3 5
Add 9	R 3 5 9
Sus4	R 3 4 5
Major 7 (M7)	R 3 5 7
Major 6 (M6)	R 3 5 6
Major 9 (M9)	R 3 5 7 9
6/9	R 3 5 6 9

Minor Family

Basic minor chord	R b3 5
Add9	R b3 5 9
Minor 6 (m6)	R b3 5 6
Minor 7 (m7)	R b3 5 b7
Minor 9 (m9)	R b3 5 b7 9
Minor 11 (m11)	R b3 5 b7 11
Minor 7b5 (m7b5)	R b3 b5 b7

7th Family

Basic 7th chord	R 3 5 b7
9th	R 3 5 b7 9
13th	R 3 5 b7 13
7#9	R 3 5 b7 #9
7b9	R 3 5 b7 b9
7#5 (augmented or aug 5th)	R 3 #5 b7
7b5	R 3 b5 b7
7b9#5	R 3 #5 b7 b9
7#9b5	R 3 b5 b7 #9

A Couple of Caveats...

Just like the major 7 chord is not to be confused with the 7th chord, the 9th chord also has multiple personalities. There are actually four different types of 9th chords that belong to different chord families, and have different applications.

The Add9 chord is simply a basic major or minor chord with the 9th degree added to it. It functions well in almost every musical context.

The major 9 (M9) chord is a major chord that includes the 7th as well as the 9th degree. This chord is in the major family, and has a much more lush sound than the Add9 chord.

The 9 chord is in the 7th family and contains the basic components of the 7th chord (R 3 5 b7) as well as the 9th degree. Don't mistake the 9th chord for a major 9th.

The minor 9 (m9) chord is a minor chord that has a flatted 7th as well as the 9th degree.

The following examples show some fairly common chords, and how they are created by inserting the numeric scale degrees that the chord calls for. Just as with the sus4 and add9 chords, when a chord has an extended name, like A13, or BbM9, you simply locate that numeric value of the scale, and add it to the original chord.

Sometimes, when you add additional notes to a basic chord, you have to relinquish one of the original chord tones. The fifth degree is often expendable in that it doesn't really define a chord. The root tells you the key, the third tells you if it's major or minor, and the 7th tells you if it's seventh chord. The fifth is a note that adds harmony to the chord, but if removed, the chord will not lose its character. Occasionally other chord tones are also omitted.

9th Chords (R 3 5 b7 9)

Here is an a 9th chord carved out of an A form scale. The 9th, is in the upper octave of the scale. The 9th is a 2nd one octave higher.

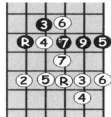

Here is an a 9th chord extracted from an E form scale. While this is a very useful chord, it is one of the rare chord voicings that omits the root, which silently resides on the sixth string.

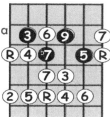

13h Chords (R 3 5 b7 13)

Here is an a 13th chord extracted from an E form scale. As shown on the previous page, a 13th chord is in the seventh family of chords, with the 13th degree of the scale added to it. The 13th is actually the sixth, but an octave above the root.

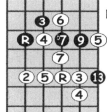

Here is a 13th chord carved out of an E form scale. As with the previous chord, You can see how the 13th trumped the 5th.

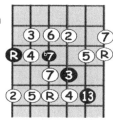

7#9 and 7b9 Chords (R 3 5 b7 #9 and R 3 5 b7b9)

This variation of a seventh chord shows up a lot in jazz, but listen to the first chord in the Jimi Hendrix tune, Purple Haze.

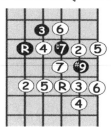

This #9 and b9 chords are often used together, toggling the #9 and b9 notes to create motion within the chord.

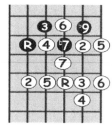

Minor7b5 Chords R b3 b5 b7

This chord appears a lot in jazz and pop tunes and is worth putting in your chordal toolbox.

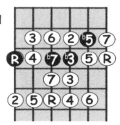

This chord has the same fingering as the 9th chord shown above, but you can see that since the root is in a different place, it is used in a different melodic context. When two chords have the same fingering, but are in different families, they are called enharmonic. Same notes—different context.

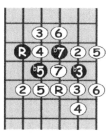

More on Extended Chords

Here is a glossary of some of the more sophisticated chord forms that populate the three chord families. A lot of them will not have a lot of utility unless you plan on exploring jazz, but just understanding the chord/scale relationships, and how they relate to the three chord families will make you a much more enlightened guitarist.

Notice that some of these chords were introduced earlier in the book, but are fingered differently here. There is rarely just one way to play a given chord, since you generally have the same scale degrees repeating in the chord. Knowing where the scale degrees reside enables you make choices as to how to shape a chord.

The chord symbols ae displayed with left hand fingering, with scale degrees at the bottom.

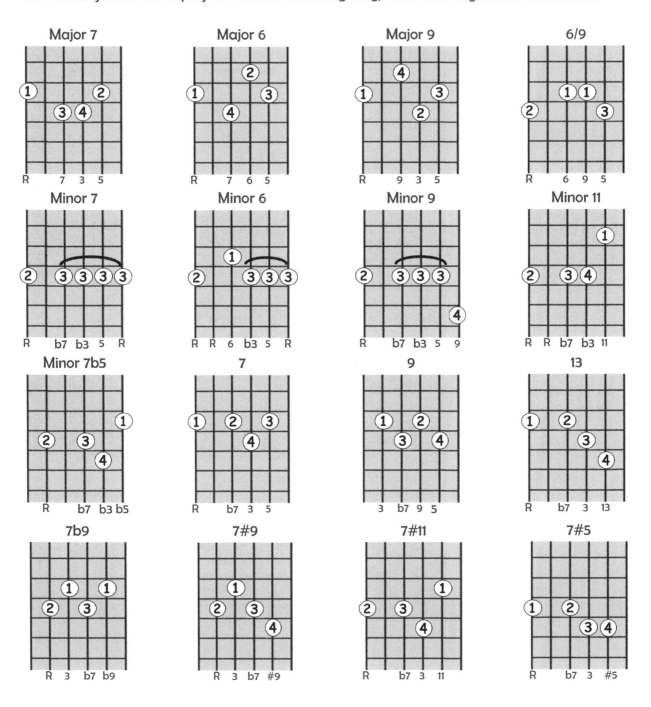

Below are two 12 bar blues progressions that illustrate how a standard chord progression can be enhanced by inserting additional chords from a given chord family. Since a blues is typically comprised of 7th chords, most of the chords in these examples are generated from that family. A few other chords were thrown in for additional color.

Example 1

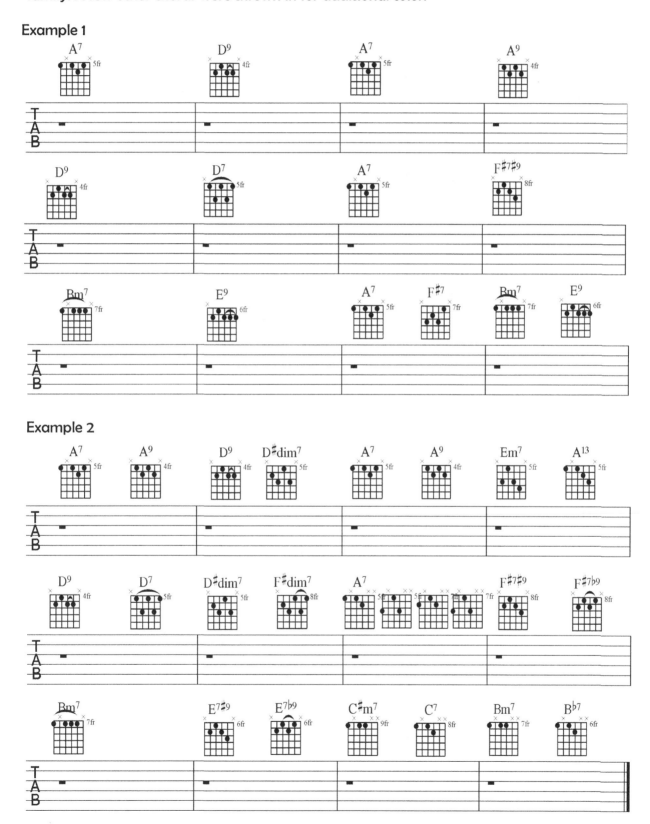

Example 2

Learning Songs By Ear

Learning songs visually, like from YouTube videos, is a great way to learn songs and techniques, but learning tunes "by ear" is an indispensable skill that you should learn. Developing your ear is essential to playing music, and learning songs from recordings is the best way to do that. Here's how it's done:

Find the Time Signature

Listen, and count. Try to feel the pulse of the song. Does it have 3 or 4 beats per measure? Most songs will have 4 beats per measure, but it's not uncommon for a song to have 3 beats per measure. Songs can have 6, or 9, or any number of beats per measure, but most songs will have 3 or 4.

Find the Key

The first chord in the song usually tells you the song's key. If the first chord and the last chord are not the same, the last chord in the song will usually give you the key.

As you listen to the song, play consecutive notes up and down the 6th string, and listen for the note that best matches the first or last chord in the song. Be prepared to play the beginning (or end) of the song many times while you do this.

Find the Chords

When you find the note that resonates with that first or last chord, you will have the root of that chord. Play the chord, and see if it matches the first or last chord of the song. If it does, you have established the song's key. This chord will most likely be the 1 chord of the key.

Once you have the 1 chord, refer to the chart of keys on pg. 13, and get the 4, 5 and 6 chords for that key. Many songs are built around the 1, 4, 5 and 6m chords. The 1 and 4 chords are typically major, the 5 chord is often a 7th chord, and the 6 chord is typically minor, but not always. Songs also can utilize the 2, 3 and 7 chords, and they can appear as major, minor, or 7th chords, so be prepared to listen really hard.

Major chords have a nice easy sound. Minor chords have a sad, melancholy sound, and 7th chords sound a little edgy, or unresolved. Music is all about tension and resolution with different chords having a natural "pull" towards other chords. The 1 chord will often set up the 4 chord, which pulls towards the 5 chord, which resolves to the 1 chord. Minor chords pull to seventh chords, and resolve to major chords.

Now, you have to determine when the chords change. When you discern a chord change, try to insert the 4 or 5 chord. If they don't sound right, try the 6, 3, or 2 chords. There's a good chance that you will get a match. Listen, and experiment. It gets exponentially easier after you have learned a couple of tunes this way.

If you find that the song begins with a minor chord, it can mean a couple of things. Sometimes songs start on the 6^m or the 2^m of the key, and sometimes the song is in a minor key. If a song is in a minor key, you still will find that the 1, 4 and 5 chords will be used, but the 1 and 4 chords are likely to be minor chords, and the 5 chord will be a 7th chord.

Using The Capo

Most pop, country, folk or rock tunes that are performed on the guitar are played in guitar friendly keys ie: G, C, A, E, and D. If you went through the process of identifying the key, and discovered that a song is in Bb, or C#, there's a good chance that the guitarist was using a capo. The capo allows you to play guitar friendly chords in keys that don't contain guitar friendly chords. If you can play moveable chords up and down the neck, it shouldn't be too difficult to find the 1, 4 and 5 chords in any key. Refer to page 18 to help you find the correct fret to use the capo.

Take bluegrass music. Bluegrass guitarists almost always play in the key of G because there are some guitar tricks, like the G run, that only really work in the key of G. If a song is in the key of A, a bluegrass guitarist will often put a capo on the second fret, and play in the key of G. The actual pitch of the song will be in the key of A, and while the actual chords will be A, D and E, the guitarist will still be able to get the trademark sounds of the G, C and D chords.

If you have determined that a song in the key of B, and you want to play in a guitar friendly key, say the key of G, put a capo on the fret that will allow the root of an open G chord to be a B note. B is on the 7th fret of the 6th string, so put the capo on the fourth fret, and the root of the G chord will land on the B note.

Artists will sometimes tune their guitar down a half step to make it easier to sing in guitar friendly keys, so when you watch them play familiar chords, they won't match when you play. Using a capo can help you match the visual with the audio.

The capo chart on pg. 18 will give you a quick reference as to where to put the capo for non-guitar friendly keys.

Modulation

You will find that occasionally a song will change keys. Changing keys in the middle, or end of a song can create a beautiful uplifting dynamic. Once a song modulates to a new key, the structure of the song stays the same; it's just in a different key. Songs can modulate by going up a half step, or a whole step. The last chorus of Taylor Swift's Love Story, is a good example of modulating up a whole step. Songs can also modulate to any key by stating the 5 chord of the new key, then slipping into the song's form.

Song Form

Being aware of song form is important. You need to be able to identify the verse, chorus and bridge of a song, and in some cases an intro, pre-chorus, or ending section. It will be easier to find the chords if you learn each section separately. Once you have a verse and a chorus, they will repeat throughout the song.

Verses and choruses are usually eight measures long, and songs typically follow a verse, verse, chorus format. Many songs have a pre-chorus, which is usually four bars long, and sets up the chorus. Songs can also have a bridge, which is a four or eight-measure sequence that appears once in a song, usually after an instrumental solo, or right before the last verse/chorus.
The verse, chorus, and bridge while generally staying in the same key, will follow different chord sequences, and if you can identify the different sections of a song, it will be easier to hear the chords. An intro occurs at the beginning of the song, and can be 2, 4, or 8 bars long, and is generally not repeated. An ending, or outro section, called a coda, can be of varying lengths. There are many ways to construct a song, but the verse generally starts on the 1 chord, choruses on the 1 or 4 chord, and the bridge on the 6 chord. But not always... So, listen, and experiment.

Write it Down

As you are finding the chords in a song, it's a good idea to write them down. Use the blank music sheet on the next page, and insert the chords as they appear in the tune.

Before you actually write the chords in, you may want to listen to the song, and simply make a mark in each measure where you hear a chord change. Once you know where the chords should be inserted rhythmically, you can start figuring out what the chords actually are, and write their names in the places you have notated for them.

Song Template

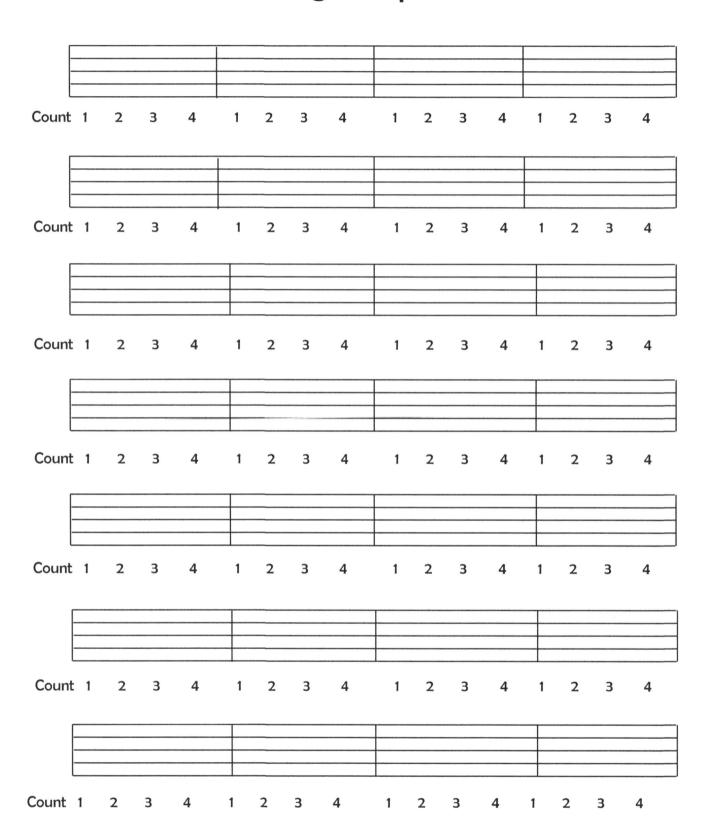

Count 1   2   3   4   1   2   3   4   1   2   3   4   1   2   3   4

Count 1   2   3   4   1   2   3   4   1   2   3   4   1   2   3   4

Count 1   2   3   4   1   2   3   4   1   2   3   4   1   2   3   4

Count 1   2   3   4   1   2   3   4   1   2   3   4   1   2   3   4

Count 1   2   3   4   1   2   3   4   1   2   3   4   1   2   3   4

Count 1   2   3   4   1   2   3   4   1   2   3   4   1   2   3   4

Count 1   2   3   4   1   2   3   4   1   2   3   4   1   2   3   4

The Songs

The songs in this section are all displayed using the number system. Use the number system to choose the key that you want to play in.

You should try to use different strums, accompaniment patterns, and moveable chords that you have learned. You also can use the capo to experiment with other keys. It's not a bad idea to write out the notes from the key (pg. 13) next to the song that you're learning, as a reference.

Be sure to observe the designation for chord types.

Lower case m = minor chord
Upper case M = major chord
7 = 7th chord
b (flat) before a chord = lower the chord a half step (one fret)

If there is no m, M or 7 designation, the chord will be a major chord.

How to Read The Chord Charts

In many songs you play two verses, then a chorus. Often the last chord in the 2nd verse is different from the 1st verse, but all of the other chords remain the same. To avoid having to write out the verse two times, a system of 1st and 2nd endings can be employed.

In a tune that employs a 1st / 2nd ending, you will see a double line with two dots at the beginning of the verse. This indicates where you return to after the first ending. Play through the song until you see a bracket above the staff with the number one. This is the 1st ending. Play until you see the double lines with 2 dots, and then return to the beginning of the tune where the first double lines are shown.

Play through the form again, but this time, bypass the measures of the 1st ending, and continue playing through the 2nd ending, and through the rest of the song.

The repeat sign does not have to be accompanied by a 1st and 2nd ending. Often, a section of the song just needs to be repeated. So, whenever you see the double dot symbol, it means repeat the section that is bracketed by these signs.

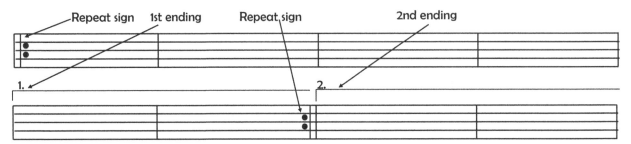

Sometimes more than one chord will appear in a measure. Most often the 2nd chord will typically be played on the 3rd beat but, you will find some tunes where additional chords may occur on any beat. The song charts in the next section will show the counts below any measure where more than one chord occurs, so you will know on which beat to strum.

The following example shows some of the possible chord designations you will encounter.

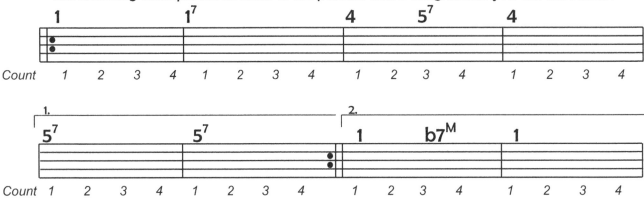

If the song was in the key of G, the 1st measure would contain a G major chord, the 2nd measure, a G7 chord, the 3rd measure a C and D7 chord, played on the 1st and 3rd beat respectively. The 4th measure would contain a C chord.

The 5th and 6th measures are bracketed as the first ending with a D7 chord. Return to the beginning of the song (observe the double dot, double bar symbol), and continue to the 2nd ending.

The $b7^M$ on the 3rd beat of the 7th measure would be an F major. The 7th degree in the key of G is an F#. The b (flat) sign in front of it tells you to lower the chord a half step, making it an F, and the M after the 7 tells you to play it as a major chord.

Blue Eyes Crying In The Rain

Brown Eyed Girl

Verse

Chorus

Come Together

Verse

Come As You Are

Verse

6^m	5	6^m	5

Chorus

2^m	4	2^m	4

Crazy

Verse

1	6^M	2^m 6^M	2^m

5^7	5^7	1. 1 6^M	2^m 5^7

Chorus

2. 1	4	1	4	4

1^M	1^M	2^M	2^M

5^7 2^M	5^7	1	6^M

2^m 6^M	2^m	4 3^m	2^m 3^m

2^m 5^7	1 (5)		

Dock of The Bay

Dock of The Bay

| 1 Verse | 3⁷ | 4 | 2ᴹ |

| 1 | 3⁷ | 4 | 2ᴹ |

| 1 Chorus | 2ᴹ | 1 | 2ᴹ |

| 1 | 2ᴹ | 1 | 2ᴹ |

Bridge

| 1   5 | 4 | 1   5 | 4 |

| 1   5 | 4 | b7ᴹ | 5 |

Don't Stop Believing

| 1 Verse | 5 | 6ᵐ | 4 |

| 1 | 5 | 4 | 4 |

| 1 Chorus | 5 | 6ᵐ | 4 |

| 1 | 5 | 4 | 4 |

| 4 Bridge | 4 | 1 | 1 |

| 4 | 4 | 5 | 5 |

Don't Think Twice, It's All Right

| 1 | 5 | 6^m | 6^m |

1 | 5 | 6^m | 6^m

4 | 4 | 1 | 5

1 | 5 | 6^m | 6^m

2^M | 2^M | 5 | 5

1 | 1 | 1^7 | 1^7

4 | 4 | 2^M | 2^M

1 | 5 | 6^m | 4

To repeat the form play the 5 chord here. Otherwise, just end the song on the 1 chord. **(5)**

1 | 5 | 1 | 1

Dust in The Wind

1 Verse | 5 | 6^m | 6^m

5 | 2^m | 6^m | 6^m

2 Chorus | 5 | 6^m | 6^m

Every Breath You Take

Verse

| 1 | 1 | 6^m | 6^m |

| 4 | 5 | 6^m | 6^m |

Chorus

| 4 | $b3^M$ | 1 | 1 |

| 2^M | 2^M | 5 | 5 |

Verse

| 1 | 1 | 6^m | 6^m |

| 4 | 5 | 6^m | 6^m |

Bridge

| $b6^M$ | $b6^M$ | $b7^M$ | $b7^M$ |

| $b6^M$ | $b6^M$ | $b7^M$ | $b7^M$ |

| $b6^M$ | $b6^M$ | 1 | 1 |

| 6^m | 6^m | 4 | 5 |

| 6^m | 6^m | | |

Folsom Prison Blues

Free Bird

Friend of The Devil

Verse

1	5	6	5	4	1	5	1

5 Chorus

5	5	2^m	4

5	5	5	5

5 Bridge

4	4	4	4

Get Back

1 Verse

1	4	1

1	1	4	1

1 Chorus

1	1	4	1	$b7^M$ 4

1	1	4	1	$b7^M$ 4

Halleleuia

| 1 | 1 | 6^m | 6^m |

| 1 | 1 | 6^m | 6^m |

| 4 | 4 | 5 | 5 |

| 1 | 1 | 5 | 5 |

| 1 | 1 | 4 | 5 |

| 6^m | 6^m | 4 | 4 |

| 5 | 5 | 3⁷ | 3⁷ |

| 6^m | 6^m | 6^m | 6^m |

| 4 | 4 | 4 | 4 |

| 6^m | 6^m | 6^m | 6^m |

| 4 | 4 | 4 | 4 |

| 1 | 1 | 5 | 5 |

Interlude

| 1 | 1 | 6^m | 6^m |

| 1 | 1 | 6^{'''} | 6^{'''} |

Heart of Gold

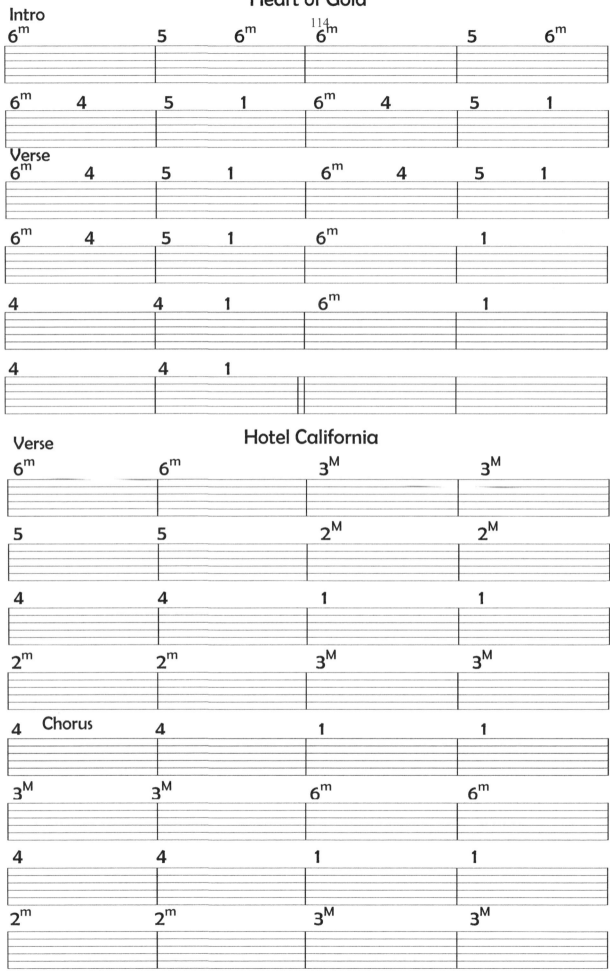

House of The Rising Sun

6^m	6^m	1	1	115

2^M	2^M	4	4

6^m	6^m	1	1

3^M	3^M	3^M	3^M

6^m	6^m	1	1

2^M	2^M	4	4

6^m	6^m	3^M	3^M

1	1

I'm Yours

1 Verse	1	5	5

6^m	6^m	4	4

1 Chorus	1	5	5

6^m	6^m	4	4

1 Bridge	5	6	5

4	4	2^7	2^7

I Heard it Through The Grapevine

1ᵐ	1ᵐ	5	4

6ᵐ	4	1ᵐ	4

1ᵐ	1ᵐ	5	5

1ᵐ	1ᵐ	5	5

1ᵐ	1ᵐ	1ᵐ	1ᵐ

I Walk The Line

5	5	1	1

5	5	1	1

4	4	1	1

5	5	1	1

Knocking On Heavens Door

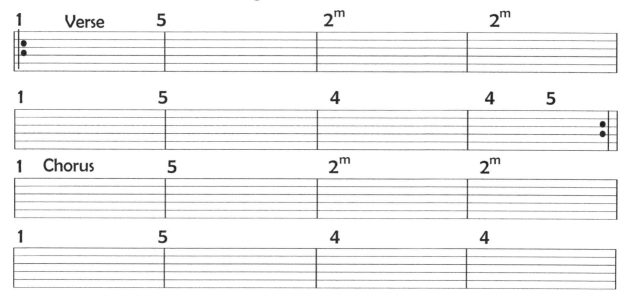

1 Verse	5	2^{m}	2^{m}

1	5	4	4 5

1 Chorus	5	2^{m}	2^{m}

1	5	4	4

Landslide

1 Verse 4x	1/3	2^{m7}	1/3

1	1/3	4 5	

1 Chorus	1/3	6^{m}	1/3

4	4/7	2^{m7}	5

Lay Down Sally

1 Intro	b7^M	1	b7^M

1 Verse	1	1	1

1.

2.

4	4	4	4

5 Chorus	5	1	1

4	4	5	5

1	b^{7M}	1	1

4	4	5	5

1	b^{7M}	1	b^{7M}

Leaving On A Jet Plane

1M7	4M7	1M7	4M7

1	6m	5	5

Let It Be

1 Verse	5	6m	4

1	5	4	1

6m Chorus	5	4	1

1	5	4	1

Love Story

1 Verse	1	4	4

6m	6m	4	4

4	5	1	1

4	4	5	5

1 Chorus	1	5	5

6m	6m	4	5	(1)

Last chorus played 2 frets higher. End song on the 1 chord.

Let it Go

6^m Verse 3x	4	5	2^{7sus4} 2^m

6^m	5	2	2

5 Pre Chorus	5	4	4

5	5	4	4

1 Chorus 3x	5	6^m	4

3^m	$^b3$	4	4

4 Bridge	4	4	4

4	4	4	4

5	5	5	5

6^m	4	5	2^m 4

1 Chorus 3x	5	6^m	4

3^m	$^b3$	4	4

Margaritaville

1 Verse   **1**   **1**   **1**

1   **1**   **5**   **5**

5   **5**   **5**   **5**

5   **5**   **1**   **1**

4 Chorus   **5**   **1**   **1**

4   **5**   **1**   **1**

4   **5**   **1**   **5**   **4**

4   **5**   **1**   **1**

My Girl

1 Verse   **4**   **1**   **4**

1   **4**   **1**   **4**

1   **2^m**   **4**   **5**   **1**   **2^m**   **4**   **5**

1   **4**   **1**   **5**

No Woman No Cry

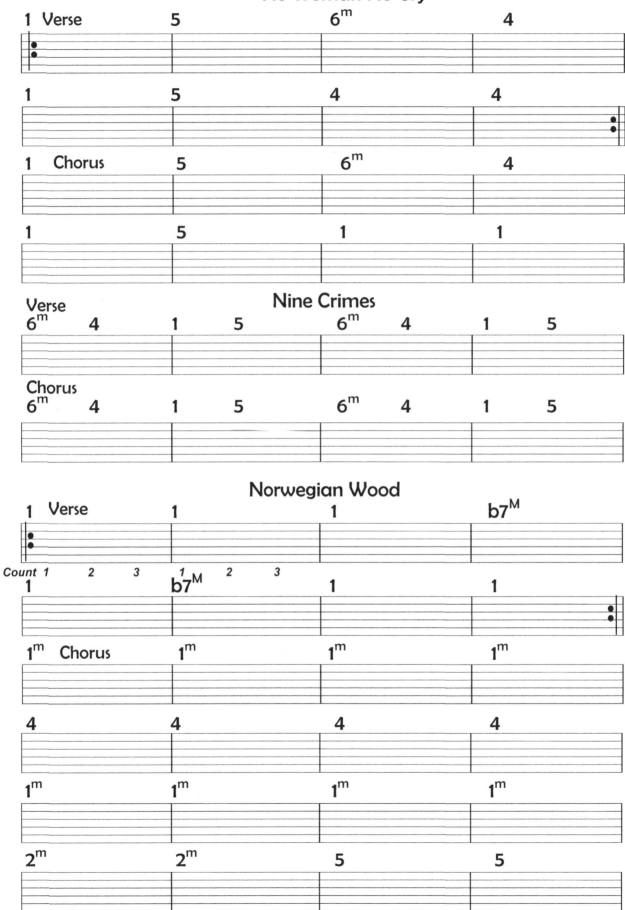

One Love

1 Chorus	1	5	5

4	1	5	1

1 Verse	6^m	4	1

1	6^m	4 5	1

Over The Rainbow

1	6^m	3^m 5^1	4	1 1^7

1.

4 4^m	1	6^m 2^m 5^7	1 2^m 5^7

2.

4 4^m	1	6^m 2^m 5^7	1

1 1^{Ma7} 1^{Maj6} 1^{Maj7}	4 4^{Ma7} 4^{Maj6} 4^{Maj7}	2^m 5^7	1

1 1^{Ma7} 1^{Maj6} 1^{Maj7} 1^{dim}	2^m	5^7 5$^{7 aug}$	

1	6^m	3^m 5^1	4	1 1^7

4 4^m	1	6^m 2^m 5^7	1

Ring of Fire

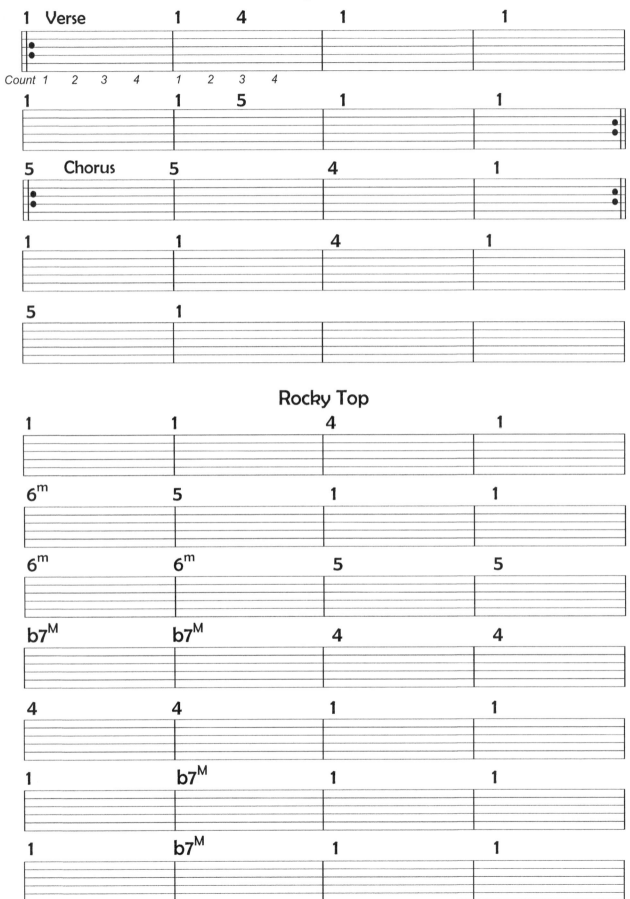

Rocky Top

Roll In My Sweet Baby's Arms

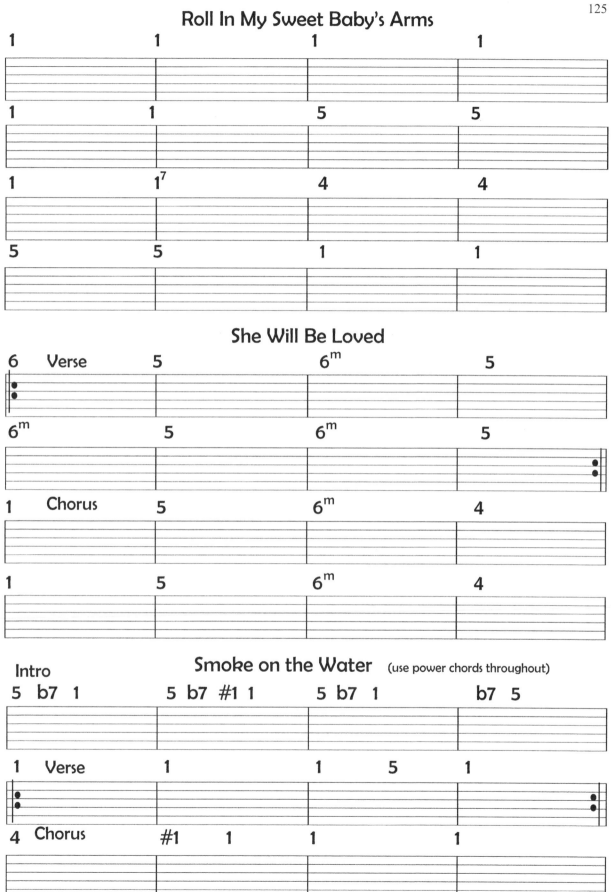

She Will Be Loved

Smoke on the Water (use power chords throughout)

126

Snow (Hey oh)

Something

Stand By Me

1 Verse	1	6^m	6^m

4	5	1	1

1 Chorus	1	6^m	6^m

4	5	1	1

Sweet Child of Mine

1 Verse	1	$b7^M$	$b7^M$

4	4	1	1

5 Chorus	$b7^M$	1	1

5	$b7^M$	1	1

2^m Solo	$b7^M$	6^7	5^m

2^m Outro	4	5	$b7^M$ 3^M End on 2^M

3 beats per measure

Sweet Baby James

128

Intro

| 4 | 1/3 | 2^m | 5^{7}sus | 5^7 |

| 1 Verse | 5 | 4 | 3^m |

Count *1   2   3   1   2   3*

| 3^m | 6^m | 4 | 1 |

| 3^m | 3^m | 6^m | 4 |

| 1 | 3^m | 4 | 1 |

| 5 | 2^m | 2^m | 5^7 |

| 5^7 | 4 | 4 | 5 |

| 1 | 6^m | 4 | 1 |

| 5 | 6^m | 4 | 5 |

| 1 | 6^m | 4 | 1 |

| 1 | 2^M | 2^M | 5$^{7\ sus4}$ |

| 5$^{7\ sus4}$ | 5^7 | 5^7 | 1 Chorus |

| 4 | 5 | 1 | 6^m |

| 4 | 1 | 1 | 6^m |

| 4 | 1 | 1 | 2^M |

| 2^M | 5^7 | 5^7 | 4 |

| 5 | 1 | 1 | |

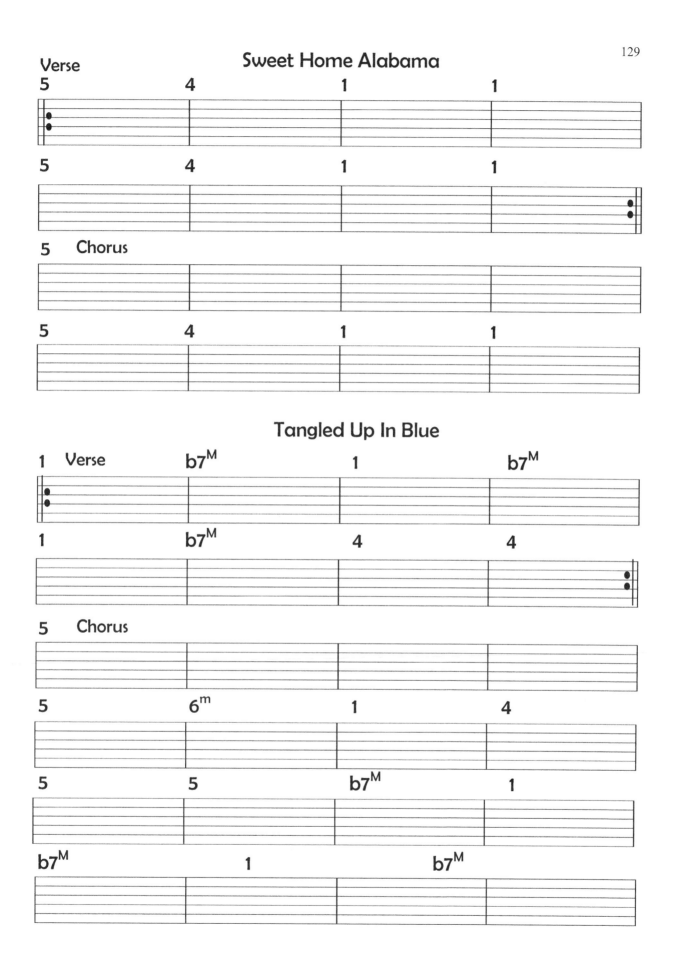

Take Me Home Country Roads

1 Verse   **1**   **6**^{m} **6**^{m}

5   **5**   **4**   **1**

1 Chorus   **1**   **5**   **5**

6^m **6**^{m} **4**   **4**

1   **1**   **5**   **5**

4   **4**   **1**   **1**

6^m Bridge   **5**   **1**   **1**

4   **1**   **5**   **5**

6^m **b7**^{M} **4**   **1**

5   **5**   **5**   **5**

1 Chorus   **1**   **5**   **5**

6^m **6**^{m} **4**   **4**

1   **1**   **5**   **5**

4   **4**   **1**   **1**

Teach Your Children

Verse

1	1	4	4

1	1	5	5

Chorus

1	1	4	4

1	1	5	5

1	1	4	4

1	1	6^m	6^m 5

4	5	1	1

Teardrops on My Guitar

Verse

1	6^m	4	5

4	5	4	5

1	6^m	4	5

6^m	4	1	5

Chorus

1	1	6^m	4

1	1	6^m	4

Tears in Heaven

1 Verse $\quad$ 5 $\qquad$ 6^m $\qquad$ 4 $\quad$ 1 $\qquad$ 5

6^m $\qquad$ 3^M $\qquad$ 5^m $\qquad$ 6^M

2^m $\qquad$ 5^7 $\qquad$ 1 $\quad$ 5 $\qquad$ 6^m

4 $\quad$ 5 $\qquad$ 1 $\quad$ 5 $\qquad$ $b3^M$ Bridge $b7^M$ $\qquad$ 1^m $\quad$ 4

$b7^M$ $\qquad$ $b3^M$ $\quad$ $b7^M$ $\qquad$ 1^m $\quad$ 4 $\qquad$ $b7^M$

5

The Time of Your Life

1 $\qquad$ 1 $\qquad$ 4 $\qquad$ 5

6^m $\qquad$ 5 $\qquad$ 4 $\qquad$ 1

6^m $\qquad$ 1 $\qquad$ 6^m $\qquad$ 1

6^m $\qquad$ 5 $\qquad$ 1 $\qquad$ 1

This Land Is Your Land

4 $\qquad$ 4 $\qquad$ 1 $\qquad$ 1

5 $\qquad$ 5 $\qquad$ 1 $\qquad$ 1

4 $\qquad$ 4 $\qquad$ 1 $\qquad$ 1

5 $\qquad$ 5 $\qquad$ 1 $\qquad$ 1

Wagon Wheel

Verse

1	5	6m	4

1	5	4	4

Chorus

1	5	6m	4

1	5	4	4

What Makes You Beautiful

Verse

1	4	5	1	4	5

1	4	5	1	4	5

Chorus

1	4	6m	5	1	4	6m	5

1	4	5	1	4	5

1	4	5	1	4	5

1	4	5	6m	1

Wish You Were Here

6^m Intro and Sol	1	6^m	1

6^m	2	6^m	2	1	1

4 Verse	5	2^m	1

5	4	2^m	1

With You Or Without You

1 Verse	5	6^m	4

1	5	4	1

1 Chorus	5	6^m	4

1	5	6^m	4

You Are My Sunshine

1	1	1	1

4	4	1	1

4	4	1	1

1	5	1	1

Thanks for taking the time to look at my book. I hope that the information in *Fear of Guitar* has given you some insights into playing the guitar, and provided you with tools that you can use to make music. Best of luck on your musical journey!

Peter Mealy

About the author

Peter Mealy is a guitarist, and singer who has been performing and teaching since the 1970's. He has toured extensively with his wife, and music partner, Laurie Rose Griffith.

He has won numerous awards for his songwriting, and has been a featured instrumentalist in the guitar workshops at the Philadelphia Folk Festival, and the Washington Folk Festival.

Peter is the author of *Fear of Chords, Fear of Soloing, Fear of Ukulele,* and *Melodic Fingerestyle Guitar,* and has contributed articles and columns to *Acoustic Musician* and *Bluegrass Unlimited.*

Peter and Laurie live in Fredericksburg, Virginia with their daughters, Adrian and Rosalie. He can be contacted through his website:

www.nofearbooks.com

Made in the USA
Middletown, DE
20 November 2022

15415362R00077